FRUSTRATION

Have you ever tried to talk to someone
and been frustrated in your efforts?

This book offers tools you can
use to get your point across.

FOREWORD

In a speech, Mortimer J. Adler, former professor of the
philosophy of law at the University of Chicago, said:

> It is almost impossible for any of us to use any
> words that are understood by other people in
> exactly the sense in which we use them...

> Even the most careful and precise use of
> language, which is difficult sometimes to
> accomplish, leaves the result incomplete,
> inadequate, and, often worse than that,
> something that is moving in the wrong
> direction...

> Anyone who went to school and college before
> 1900 had something that no one who goes to
> school has today. They had a common literary
> heritage...those of our ancestors who were
> educated persons had read a large number of
> books in common and this gave them a
> common vocabulary and a common background
> of ideas and references, allusions, which made
> communication between them easier.

> Today this is not true. I had this experience at
> the University of Chicago. Our teachers or our

professors cannot talk with one another. They
are all so specialized. Each of them has read or
studied or worked in such a special field of
literature, with its own technical jargon, that
communication across the lines of their
specialties is very poor. Even in certain fields,
subordinate specializations within the fields of
physics and mathematics, communication is
difficult among mathematicians and physicists,
which would not have been true two or three
hundred years ago.[1]

Adler (1902-2001) reached celebrity status with the
publication in 1952 of the 54 volume set of the *Great Books
of the Western World* by Encyclopedia Britannica, which he
co-edited with Robert M. Hutchins. He was greatly
influenced by the philosophy of Aristotle and Thomas
Aquinas and authored many books.[2]

DEDICATION

This book is dedicated to:

Saikat Guha (1976-2008)
An extraordinary mind, cut short

To learn more
turn to Appendix C

The Way Things Are Series

Book Two

TEN PRECEPTS
of
DIALOGUE

The Tools of Constructive Discourse

Charles Hoppins

Western Research Institute, Inc.

Author: Charles Hoppins
Editors: Eleanor Gibson and Ron Friedli

Published by Western Research Press
P.O. Box 45061
Boise ID 83711-5061

As of this printing, telephone
number was (208) 703-5709
email address was westernresearch@earthlink.net

Library of Congress Catalogue Number: Pending

ISBN 10 1-882567-30-7
ISBN 13 978-1-882567-30-0
The Way Things Are series: ISBN 1-882567-27-7

10, 9, 8, 7, 6, 5, 4

PREFACE

As we have seen in the "Foreword" there may be a problem
of communication *between* the various disciplines
and *within* the various disciplines. This is particularly
true *between* the disciplines of philosophy, psychology,
sociology, physics, medicine, information technology and
science; and *between* academia, the business community and
the general public.[1] And it is true *within* each of these
disciplines, and *within* the corporate world and government.

To complicate things further, there are generation gaps.
Older adults are often at a loss to understand the thinking of
younger adults. And then there is the problem of
communication in dealing with adolescence. And still
further is the problem of communication between classes,
races and cultures. It is this unholy mix of cross discourse
that this treatise seeks to address and to some extent remedy.
Part of the problem is that people do not realize there is a
problem.

On the surface, this problem of communication appears to be
a matter of terminology. Each discipline, each area of human
endeavor and each generation has created its own jargon and
unless you are immersed in a particular field or a member of
a specific generation, race or culture, you are at a
disadvantage.

Not obvious are other issues such as levels of intellection, rhetorical skill, the use of language and prejudices. In addition to this, elements of communication that relate to philosophy, mainly language, have become highly complicated and even controversial.

We are mostly concerned here with the disparities of language in and between the disciplines of philosophy, psychology and sociology and across a number of generations. This is addressed further in the Introduction.

TABLE OF CONTENTS

1. Right to Position
2. Right to State and Define Position
3. Obligation to Receive Position
4. Right to Disagree
5. Right to Verify
6. Right to Define Terms
7. Obligation to Accept Terms
8. Obligation to Distinguish
9. Obligation to Not Impute
10. Obligation to Abide by Rules of Logic

INTRODUCTION

At the beginning of the 20th Century, philosophy took a departure from tradition which has led to complications in communication and philosophical discourse. These complications are progressively dealt with in the first nine chapters. They have much to do not only with philosophy, but with the sociological impact of modernism and post modernism and to some extent developments in psychology.

Communication is a vast subject of which only a tiny part can be dealt with in a single book. This book deals only with that part of communication that relates to argumentation or dialogue. We define dialogue as *constructive discourse between two or more people about a specific subject.* By constructive discourse, we mean discourse that is *meaningful* to the parties involved and that produces greater understanding of the subject under discussion. Ultimately this means a greater understanding of truth and the way things are in reality, which includes solutions to problems and coming to terms or agreement between the parties involved.

Thus we are limiting our discussion of communication in this treatise to *dialogue* that is *meaningful* and that produces *greater understanding, solutions* and *agreement.* Thus, we distinguish it from debate, persuasion and deception. This treatise deals with philosophy only to the extent that it applies to dialogue that produces these results. And for dialogue to achieve these results it must be based on certain philosophical elements. These philosophical elements are outlined in the first chapter. They are expanded on in succeeding chapters.

Polls indicate there is substantial disagreement within the current philosophical community on the validity of certain elements of philosophy and the use of language. This is dealt with mainly in Chapters I, III, IV, V and VI.

As several philosophers have said, whenever there is disagreement on a position or state of affairs, someone is in error. What this means is there is only one reality and only one perception of that reality can be valid or true. The Ten Precepts of Dialogue are designed to provide participants in an argument the tools to come to the knowledge of the truth of any matter. Thus the Ten Precepts of Dialogue are much about truth and what makes a thing or statement true. This is dealt with in Chapter IV on The Role of Truth.

Since this work is directed at a mass audience that for the most part is not versed in philosophy, a limited review of the finer philosophical elements on the various subjects dealt with will be relegated to the end notes in Appendix B.

CHAPTER I
BASIC QUESTIONS

There are certain basic precepts or elements of philosophy that are often overlooked in various forms of communication as a result of current trends in philosophical inquiry.

Among these are the nature of general statements, the implications of the principle of contradiction and the excluded middle, the nature of reality, the implications of a negative universal, the nature of truth, the nature of proof, the role of language, the role of belief systems and the prevalence of false statements and deception.

These elements are particularly relevant to philosophical argumentation, but they also play a significant role in other forms of communication. They play a role in how we address certain issues and how we respond to certain arguments. The role these elements play is viewed differently according to various philosophical positions in opposition to each other which complicate the application of these elements to various forms of communication. These positions include objectivism as opposed to subjectivism and relativism; realism as opposed to idealism and phenomenalism; various perceptions of what constitutes truth; and empiricism versus rationalism.

Then there are approaches variously described as traditions, schools or movements such as analytic, continental, and Scholasticism, the latter of which includes Aristotelianism and Thomism. These approaches mainly consist of analytic philosophy as opposed to continental philosophy and Scholasticism. We will deal mainly with opposing positions held by analytical philosophers as opposed to mainline or traditional philosophers.

We will list and briefly explain each of these elements in this chapter. In succeeding chapters we will list and explain the pros and cons as they are viewed by different groups of philosophers and explain more fully their significance. As noted in the Introduction, since this book is directed to the general public, we will use the end notes to expand further for those interested in the finer points of philosophy. The differences of opinion vary substantially between the various elements and between philosophers. We will also review in later chapters certain problems as they relate to various forms of communication such as suppression, oppression, intimidation, deception, misdirection, illusion, delusion, obfuscation, redefinition and the intentional and unintentional misuse of words and language.

Most of us are probably acquainted with the statement:

All general statements are false, including this one. Some might call that a tautology or an oxymoron. With a slight adjustment, we can make it into a true axiom by restating it thus:

- General statements are such that they are generally not true. With that axiom in mind, we can be more readily on guard to make correct determination about a particular statement.

Another similar statement is: *You can't prove a negative universal, including this one.* Again we can restate it:

- Negative universal statements are such that they generally cannot be proven.

Some examples of negative universal statements are: There is no such thing as a basic philosophy. You can't prove external reality. The principle of identity is not valid. There is no God. All these negative statements cannot be proved. They, however, all have the potential to be disproved.

- While a negative universal statement generally cannot be proven, it can be disproved by proving the contradiction of it.

- Most professional philosophers accept as valid the distinction between external reality and internal reality. External reality is everything that exists outside the mind. Internal reality is everything that exists inside the mind.

- Since reality is the way it is, it can't be anything else. From this we can conclude there is only one reality. Since there is only one reality, there can be only one true perception of that reality and that is the correct perception.

- That is what makes a thing true: the correct perception of the way a thing is in reality. This is called the correspondence concept of truth. That is what truth is.

- From this we can conclude that since philosophy is about the correct understanding of the way things are, and since there are often many conflicting positions about the way a particular thing is in reality, only one position can be correct or true. It is possible that there is no position on a particular subject that is true. However, if there is one that is true, only that one can be true. We can further conclude that since there are contradictory positions held on nearly all philosophical positions, it is possible that some if not many of the positions held by any particular philosopher are false.

A belief system is the totality of positions within a specific entity, philosophy, religion or individual. Since there are many conflicting philosophical belief systems, only one can be true. This applies to religion and individuals as well as philosophy. Each religion and each denomination has its own belief system. Each person has two belief systems—conscious and subconscious. This is not to say that there is a particular belief system that is true. It is possible—and what is more likely—there is no belief system, whether philosophical, religious or individual, in which all the positions within a particular system are true. People, at least subconsciously, recognize this.

- When someone offers proof of something or says you can't prove something, we need to inquire into the nature of proof. When we do this, we come up with the "to whom" factor. It is the "to whom" factor that invalidates a lot of philosophical statements about proof.

- Few people have analyzed the nature of language. Most of us have not taken the time to analyze how our thoughts get translated into words, how words make up terms and how terms represent complicated ideas or concepts that get conveyed in writing and speaking. Analyzing this is the province of philosophy. And, indeed, much of the philosophizing of the past century (the 20th) has been concentrated on analyzing how this is accomplished

- Much of the information we are daily confronted with is false. This is true of information presented to us in the media, on radio and television, in newspapers and magazines, in books, on the Internet, in schools, colleges and universities, and yes, even in churches, synagogues and mosques. Discerning what is true and what is false is important. It affects what we believe about all things, our work, our family life, our spiritual life, our religion, our health, how we feel about things, what we do in certain circumstances, who we vote for, and how much money we make, among other things.

These are all elements of philosophy that two or more people have to deal with in discussing solutions to various problems and in dealing with various subjects. They are particularly relevant to philosophical argumentation or dialogue. From these elements we create tools of discourse which consist of rules or precepts of dialogue, which is the subject of the next chapter.

Chapter II is concerned with the main purpose of philosophical discourse or dialogue, which is to inform, learn, and gain in knowledge and wisdom

CHAPTER II
TOOLS OF DISCOURSE

Communicating our thoughts, desires, feelings, ideas, needs and other things is one of the most fundamental drives of human nature. How effective we are at doing this is one of the most important elements in achieving success in all our relationships involving our family, our work, our children, our social life, our intellectual life, and in our emotional well being. Some people are naturally good at it. Some people have no clue, or so it would seem to those of us who think we do have a clue.

Communication is a broad term encompassing body language, nuances and other forms of expression. Here we are concerned only with verbal or written communication, the use of language, so to speak. Language has many uses. These uses include: to exhort, command, inform, persuade and entertain. It is also used to confuse and deceive. As stated in the introduction, in this treatise we are limiting our discussion to dialogue. We have defined dialogue as *constructive discourse between two or more people about a specific subject.*

This chapter is concerned with the main purpose of philosophical discourse or dialogue, which is to inform, learn, and gain in knowledge and wisdom. In philosophical discourse or dialogue we will seek to enhance our understanding of the way things are in reality. A deviant use of philosophical discourse is to advance a cause or an agenda which involves political correctness, winning an argument or persuasion. We will not deal extensively here with winning an argument or persuasion. The distinction between the two is dealt with in Chapter IX and X..

To effectively communicate a position, we need some standard. There is a minimum standard like I send and you receive and then you send and I receive and hope what I send you receive and not something else and vice versa. All too often the understanding of what is sent by the sender is different than what is perceived by the receiver. It is one way the truth gets distorted or a statement or position becomes false. It is how conflicts often arise.

To make philosophical arguments and other forms of communication meaningful and productive we need to put in place certain rules and certain standards. Thus this book is about what we will label "meaningful communication." To make philosophical arguments meaningful we need some tools of discourse. We have reviewed much that has been written about rules of various forms of discourse, the *new rhetoric,* the use of language, metalinguistics, metacommunication and elements of philosophy as they relate to communication, and have incorporated important elements into this treatise.

MAKING DISCOURSE MEANINGFUL

Out of all these elements of communication, we have created Ten Precepts of Dialogue which we will apply to philosophical discourse to make it *meaningful.*

Meaningful communication is that special kind of dialogue that should take place when arguing philosophical positions. Unfortunately, arguing philosophical positions is all too often not *meaningful* or productive.

This book was written in response to arguments over a half century in which definitions were de-emphasized, logical rules violated and certain positions unfairly denigrated.

It is difficult to maintain an argument when you don't have a right to your position. It is difficult to put forth a position when you don't have a right to define the terms you use to explain a position. It is difficult to engage in meaningful communication when one of the parties employs fallacies and illogical statements in presenting and/or refuting a position. It is difficult to accept when one of the parties persists with the fallacy of "Invincible Ignorance."

It is less difficult if you have a communicators "Bill of Rights." The Ten Precepts of Dialogue are the inalienable rights guaranteed to everyone who wishes to engage in *Meaningful Communication*. They are best applied when anyone purports to engage in philosophical arguments. If a person doesn't agree with one or more of these precepts, then that is the first issue to be resolved.

In philosophical discourse we are mainly interested in communicating thoughts or ideas. To communicate ideas, we use terms. Terms represent images or ideas in the mind and are composed of one or more words. For terms to convey images or ideas they must have meaning. For ideas to have meaning, they must be explained or defined so that every person involved in *meaningful communication* has the same understanding of what is meant. We will expand on the significance of this in Chapter VI. Thus through constructive argumentation we can arrive at truths to which we would otherwise not attain.

What a person believes or holds on a particular matter or issue we call his point of view or position. The first or proximate objective of *meaningful communication* is to reach agreement on a particular position or issue between two or more people and it involves three steps. In the first step, agreement does not entail whether a particular position is right or wrong, true or false. The agreement at this point entails a common understanding of what a particular position is.

Once there is agreement on the precise point or points at issue in a position, the next step is to determine whether there is agreement or disagreement on the truth or falsity of the points in question. If the parties agree, the objective is accomplished and we can proceed to the next issue. If the parties disagree, the final objective is to reach agreement on the precise points of disagreement and, in effect, agree to disagree. Through this process we can all achieve a better understanding of the way things are in reality as well as other people's understanding of it and on any other issue. This process is exemplified in law in which the first step in resolving lawsuits is bringing the subject or subjects (facts) and applicable law under dispute "at issue."

The most critical task then in achieving common ground in *meaningful communication* is that we have a common understanding of what we are talking about. Abiding by the Ten Precepts of Dialogue will go a long ways toward assuring us of that understanding. The Ten Precepts of Dialogue are the communicator's "Bill of Rights" so to speak, which encompass our ground rules for *meaningful communication*. They are just common-sense rules for philosophical discourse. To simplify them we will refer to the person holding a position as the "communicator." We will refer to the person or persons to whom a position is being proffered as the communicatee(s). The ways the Ten Precepts may be used in discourse are listed in italics below each precept

The Ten Precepts of Dialogue are:

I. Everybody has a right to his position and to change it and the right to raise an issue (make a statement).

I (the communicator) have a right to my position.

I have a right to change my position.
I have a right to raise an issue.

II. Any communicator has the right to state and define a position and the obligation to defend a position or statement(s) (provide proof of their truth or validity).

I (the communicator) have the right to state and define my position.

I (the communicator) must (I have the obligation to) provide proof of the truth of my statement and/or the validity of my position.

III. The persons being communicated to (the communicatees) have the obligation to themselves, to the person making a statement or maintaining a position and to society to correctly understand and accept the statement or position being communicated.

You (the communicatee) must (You have the obligation to) understand and accept my position and/or statement (that it is legitimate).

This also gives the right of the communicatee to question the communicator.

IV. Any person has a right to disagree with the position and/or statement of any other person and to question that person.

You (the communicatee) have a right to disagree with me.
I (the communicator) have a right to disagree with you.
I have a right to question you and you have a right to question me.

V. The person maintaining a position has a right to verify that all his statements and his position are correctly understood.

I (the communicator) have a right to verify that you understand what I am saying.

VI. The person making a statement or maintaining a position has the obligation and the right to distinguish and define (within the rules of logic) the terms and concepts he uses.

I (the communicator) have the right to define the terms and concepts I use in explaining my position.

VII. All those involved in *dialogue* have the obligation to accept and use the terms and concepts as defined by the person advancing a position.

You (the communicatee) must accept my definition of the terms and concepts I use.

VIII. All parties have the obligation to distinguish between a person and the position of that person.

You (the communicatee) must distinguish between me and my position and the statements I make..

IX. All parties have the obligation to not impute to another person beliefs, knowledge, ignorance, feelings, thoughts, intentions, positions or any other thing.

You have no right to impute (that particular thing).

X. All parties have the obligation to abide by certain principles of reality, the laws of thought and certain principles and rules of logic and identification of fallacies.

You must abide by (state a particular principle, rule, law or fallacy).

These 10 precepts will be belabored in detail in Chapter IX. There are many ways they may be used to enhance dialogue. This will be the subject of Chapter XI.

CHAPTER III
THE ROLE OF PHILOSOPHY

Our belief systems are what create reality...[1]

Each of us create the things we see and hear and touch....[2]

There are two philosophical principles, the understanding of which are critical to the production of constructive results in philosophical dialogue between two or more people. Before dwelling on these, a little background is in order.

There are many systems of philosophy. The most well-known systems are those constructed by Plato and Aristotle. Both built on systems promulgated by earlier Greek philosophers. As stated previously, we will use the term "belief system" to denote the totality of positions held by a particular philosopher or philosophy. A "belief system" can also apply to the totality of an individual's conscious and subconscious beliefs. A belief system does not create reality.[3]

And so down through the ages each succeeding generation of philosophers built succeeding belief systems by making certain alterations to the systems of their predecessors. Theoretically any system of philosophy must be built on certain basic principles, assumptions or positions. And the totality of positions of any belief system can theoretically be logically traced back to certain principles, assumptions or positions on which a particular philosophical belief system is based.

Aristotle established the principle of contradiction as the first principle on which his philosophical belief system is based. Generally, succeeding generations of philosophers accepted this first principle and built their philosophical belief systems accordingly.

Rene Descartes in the 17th Century built his philosophical belief system on his famous dictum cogito ergo sum, I think, therefore I am. This split succeeding philosophical thinking into two parts, idealism and realism.[4] Still, he accepted the principle of contradiction as a valid principle as did nearly all the philosophers succeeding him—until the 20th Century.

As time progressed, philosophical belief systems fragmented and multiplied. Now there are almost as many philosophical belief systems as there are professional philosophers. The American Philosophical Association says it has 10,000 members. It is the de facto representative of philosophers in the United States and Canada. It also lists the average salaries of philosophy professors with various degrees. The average salaries of philosophy professors with a Ph.D. were listed as being compensated at substantially more than $100,000.[5] The Philosophical Documentation Center lists some 28,000 members in over 130 countries. Of course that is only the number registered. The actual number is probably much greater. And of course that doesn't mean there are that many belief systems, since many hold similar beliefs and many more have not made up their minds.

Still preliminary polling indicates that the majority of professional philosophers, mainly professors and graduate students, accept as valid the principle of contradiction and the principle of the excluded middle. There appears to be confusion about the principle of identity. There is debate about the distinction between exterior reality and interior reality.[6]

A number of professional philosophers will argue against the validity of one or more of these precepts.

For now we will deal with four precepts, which the majority of the current philosophical community appear to favor as valid although many are not all that familiar with them, according to preliminary results of polling. It has been pointed out that counting *cabbages* (heads) is not the way to arrive at the validity of any philosophical position, which is obviously correct. However, this book is about reporting as well as about the validity of the above philosophical positions and finding solutions to problems of communication.[7] And polling of professional philosophers is important because it is an indication of what the younger generation is being taught.

The two philosophical principles that are critical to dialogue are the distinction between exterior reality and interior reality and the principle of contradiction.

What we want to elaborate on first is the distinction between exterior reality, everything that exists outside the mind, and interior reality, everything that exists inside the mind.

THE GREAT DISTINCTION

We are elevating this distinction to a principle, which we will label the *great distinction*.[8] Much of philosophical discourse since Descartes has to do with reality and our ability to perceive the way things are in reality. The *great distinction* is important because it is critical in resolving the problem of universal concepts, about which there is a great deal of debate within the philosophical community.
Universal concepts are important because they have much to do with how words and terms are used—the use of language, so to speak.

The purpose of philosophy is to keep the world in confusion and philosophy professors on the gravy train, or so it would seem to many who are confronted with some of today's philosophical *arguments*. The gravy train is relative.

Philosophy today is much like exploring strange new worlds with the Starship Enterprise. One does not know what one is likely to encounter. How did this come about? There are two important figures that shaped much of philosophical thought in the 20th Century. One was Ludwig Josef Johann Wittgenstein. The Other was Bertrand Russell. Wittgenstein (1889-1951) maintained the proper subject of philosophical inquiry consisted of analysis of language. In recent informal polls, Wittgenstein and Russell were ranked first and second respectively as the most important philosophers of the last 20th Century.

So far as Wittgenstein is concerned, the only legitimate role philosophers play is in dispelling the confusions generated by applying the rules of one language-game to another. This is called ordinary language analysis. The sole concern of philosophical analysis is to root out the *source* of philosophical confusion. Once it is understood that that source is one of confused use of language, then it becomes apparent that there is no (and are no) philosophical (which means metaphysical) problems concerning any "thing" in "this here" world.[9]

Thus Wittgenstein ruled out the existence of metaphysics and ontology as legitimate philosophical subjects. It will be our position that in concentrating on language he evidently didn't understand the use of words.[10]

The other important figure is Bertrand Arthur William Russell (1872-1970) who received the Nobel Prize for literature in 1950. He is held in high regard as a brilliant mathematician. He maintained, generally speaking, that there was nothing in philosophy of which one could be certain. In his book entitled *The Problems of Philosophy*, Russell wrote:

> ...the value of philosophy must not depend upon any supposed body of definitely ascertainable knowledge to be acquired by those who study it.
>
> The value of philosophy is, in fact, to be sought largely in its very uncertainty... Thus, while diminishing our feeling of certainty as to what things are, it greatly increases our knowledge as to what they may be; it removes the somewhat arrogant dogmatism of those who have never travelled into the region of liberating doubt, and it keeps alive our sense of wonder by showing familiar things in an unfamiliar aspect.[11]

We would question that doubt is liberating and that there is nothing in philosophy that one can be certain about. We also disagree with his thoughts on the value of philosophy. In fact from the time of ancient Greece up through much of the 19th Century there were few philosophers that doubted that there were basic principles that one could be absolutely certain about. These included:

- The principle of identity

- The principle of contradiction[12]

- The principle of the excluded middle

- The distinction between external reality (everything that exists outside the mind) and internal reality (everything that exists inside the mind) which we have labelled *the great distinction*.

The validity of these precepts may be questioned by some in today's philosophical community. The position that one or more of these precepts is invalid is the first issue that should be dealt with in any attempt at constructive philosophical argumentation or dialogue.

This is important also because by using the principle of contradiction, you can prove a negative statement to be false. A negative statement is such that it generally cannot be proven. But it can be proven to be false by proving a statement that contradicts it. This is discussed more fully in Chapter V, "The Nature of Proof."

The basic principles of reality are important to us in our everyday lives. We unconsciously use them in much of what we do. For nearly all of us, we are unaware that we do this or of what they are. Which means we do not always abide by them. Therefore, since these basic principles are at times violated in communicating ideas, we need to bring them to the forefront and examine them so we can know when they are violated.

For our purposes here, it will be necessary to briefly review the first four most basic principles of reality. But before we get into the most basic principles of reality we need to define what reality is.

Reality is everything that is (exists).

Everybody, at least subconsciously, accepts this. That is, if a thing exists, if it is real, it is a part of reality. The definition does not state what is real. It only states that if a thing exists in whatever form, it is a part of reality.

For the beginner to grasp this definition of reality and the principles of reality he needs to understand that we are not dealing with tangible things, but only the residue of tangible things in the mind. That is we are transcending to a different level of perception and thinking in a new dimension.

MOST BASIC PRINCIPLES

To review, the four most basic principles of reality are *the principle of identity, the principle of contradiction, the principle of the excluded middle and the principle of the great distinction.* Most professional philosophers probably accept the first three, although some might debate their relevance and many have different concepts of the principle of identity. And of the first three, there is disagreement over which is most basic, which is probably the Principle of Contradiction. But we will go with the above order.

- The principle of identity states: *What is, is and what is not, is not.*

- The principle of contradiction states: *A thing cannot be.. and not be.. at the same time and in the same respect.*

- The principle of the excluded middle states: *A thing either is.. or is not.*

- The principle of the great distinction is *the distinction between objective reality (everything outside the mind) and subjective reality (everything inside the mind).*

We will explain the principle of the great distinction first since understanding it will help to explain the other three most basic principles. To adequately explain the principle of the great distinction we have to go back to the definition of reality and divide it into objective (external) reality and subjective (internal) reality and define the two.

Objective reality is everything that exists outside the mind.

Subjective reality is everything that exists inside the mind.

This means a distinction always exists between the way things are in objective reality (outside the mind) and the way things are in subjective reality (inside the mind).

Failure to make this distinction has led many renowned philosophers into serious errors and false positions.

So, the definition of reality includes things seen and unseen, outside the mind and inside the mind. For example the definition does not affirm the existence of God. It only affirms that if God exists, He is a part of reality. Likewise if ghosts exist they are a part of reality. If they do not exist they are not a part of reality. That is, they are not a part of *objective reality*. But they are certainly a part of *subjective reality* because the term god and ghosts stirs up images of these ephemeral beings in our mind. And if they do exist in the external world, they are a part of both objective and subjective reality, albeit in different forms.

From the extrapolation of this example, we can conclude that much of reality exists both outside the mind and as a perception inside the mind. That is, it exists both as objective reality and as a perception in subjective reality. Likewise there are things in objective reality of which the mind has no image or concept (a reasonable assumption). And there are things in subjective reality that do not exist in objective reality, such as each person's stream of consciousness or random thoughts, except those thoughts of images or ideas which represent things outside the mind. When I think something like "I have a new idea for solving the energy crisis". That statement exists only in subjective reality. Now if I write that statement down on a piece of paper or word processor, like I just did, that statement now exists as symbols in objective reality. It will also exist in subjective reality in the minds of everybody who reads it.

Plato held that ideas have existence outside the mind. That is, they exist in objective reality. We hold that they are the product of thought and as such they do not exist in objective reality except as symbols on paper, sound waves of speech or audio and video recordings. The four most basic principles then, exist in writing form as symbols on paper in a word processor program. The impressions of these symbols and sound waves exist in the mind along with the universal concepts they represent.

The principle of identity, the principle of contradiction and the principle of the excluded middle are all common-sense principles.[13] It doesn't take a rocket scientist to understand them. They are immediately obvious. To understand them does entail abstract thinking, which seems to pose difficulties for some people.

These four principles form the core of a basic philosophy. They are the foundation of all the disciplines and indeed all rational thinking. There are all kinds of conclusions that can be drawn from them. There are those in the philosophical community who will not accept these principles and there are those in all walks of life who will not accept established facts as true. These people are logically invincible. No matter what the proof, no matter what the evidence, they will not accept it. They are the kind of people who belong to the Flat Earth Society. To engage in philosophical dialogue— meaningful communication—one has to accept these four basic principles. When you run up against someone who is intractable—logically invincible—this position must first be overcome.

The principle of identity says a thing is what it is. There are those who hold that the Principle of Identity is trivial and therefore not really valid. This is a fallacy of relevance. It does not address the issue of validity or to whom it is trivial. We hold that it needs to be stated as a valid principle because there are some who will say a thing is not what it is. And there are some who will use the denial of it to justify irrational behaviour.

In regard to the Principle of Contradiction, Aristotle states "we have now posited that it is impossible for anything at the same time to be and not to be, and by this means have shown that this is the most indisputable of all principles".

We can apply each of the three most basic principles to logic and draw corollaries, which are known as *laws of thought*. From the principle of identity we can draw the first law of thought. The first law of thought states:

A statement that is true.. is true.. and a statement that is false.. is false.

From the principle of identity, the first law of thought says a true statement must be true and a false statement must be false. In other words a statement says what it says.

The principle of contradiction is thought by many to be the most fundamental and important principle in all of philosophy. And it is fundamental in all of science and all of knowledge. Aristotle states "we have now posited that it is impossible for anything at the same time to be and not to be, and by this means have shown that this is the most indisputable of all principles."

There are many conclusions that can be drawn from the principle of contradiction. Among them is its corollary, the second law of thought. The second law of thought states that:

A categorical statement cannot be true and false at the same time.

The second law of thought says that a statement cannot contradict itself. A statement may appear to be both true and false if it is ambiguous. But this is the result of applying a different meaning to one or more terms in the statement.

From the principle of contradiction, we can also conclude there can be only one true belief system about specific beliefs. For example, there can be only one true philosophy (philosophical belief system) and only one true religion (religious belief system). A belief system can be applied to philosophy, religion, any discipline or any individual. It may be there are no true belief systems about specific beliefs. But if there is one that is true or mostly true and other belief systems contradict it, only that one can be true or mostly true. Belief systems are discussed in Chapter VII.

From the principle of contradiction we can also conclude the principle of the excluded middle.

The principle of the excluded middle says that a thing either exists or does not exist.

Basically the principle of the excluded middle is saying there is no other alternative. There must be existence or non-existence.

Applied to logic, we get the third law of thought:

A categorical statement is either true or not true.[14]

This means there is no other alternative. A statement has to be either true or not true. Again, for a categorical statement to appear both true and false, one or more terms must be used in an ambiguous sense. Which leads us to the subject of terms and concepts, which are covered in Chapter VI. But first we need to address the subject of truth and what makes a thing true, which we will do in the next chapter.

CHAPTER IV
THE ROLE OF TRUTH

What is truth and what makes a thing or statement true? Results of an informal poll indicate that less than 90 percent of adults can articulate a valid answer. A substantial percentage of adults confuse truth with perception or actually have the wrong concept of what truth is. Many think truth is what the Bible says. One woman's response to the poll was that truth was what George Bush says. Many think that truth depends on perception and is different for different people.

Philosophers have come up with a dozen or more different theories of what truth is. These theories include coherence, correspondence, performative, pragmatic, relativity, minimalist (deflationary), epistemic, redundancy, constructivist, semantic, identity and pluralist.[1]

Most Americans are confused about what *truth* is and what makes a thing or statement true. That is they are not consciously aware of what constitutes *truth*. Subconsciously, or unconsciously, it is a different story.

Subconsciously, everybody, or nearly everybody, has the same notion about what *truth* is. If you want to know what a person really believes, you look at how he or she acts or reacts.

We can tell what people really believe about truth by what they say. They say such things as "That is not true... You are not telling the truth... I want the truth... That person lied, he did not tell the truth... That is true" In court a witness swears on the Bible that he will tell the truth, the whole truth and nothing but the truth". The judge, the jury, the attorneys, the spectators, all know, or at least they think they know, what telling the truth amounts to.

In all these instances, everybody, or nearly everybody, has the same understanding of what truth is. That understanding consists of the accurate portrayal of events; the correct statement of facts; the correspondence in the mind of the way a thing is in reality. On the witness stand, telling the truth means to state where a defendant was at a given time. If he says he was somewhere else than where he really was is perjury. Truth does not depend on one's perception. Truth is not what the Bible says or anyone else says. The truth is the correct representation in the mind of the way a thing is in reality. Thus it does not depend on one's perception or what someone says. It can't be changed if someone does not like it. A thing is what it is and not something else and the truth about that thing reflects what it is in reality. Everybody, or nearly everybody, understands this.

THE CORRESPONDENCE THEORY OF TRUTH

This is called the correspondence concept of truth. Preliminary analysis of polls indicate that an overwhelming majority of professional philosophers who have studied the matter will accept as valid the correspondence concept of truth.[2]

Everybody talks about the truth, about what is true and not true. Yet hardly anybody can articulate what truth is. Outside of philosophers, hardly anybody bothers with consciously questioning what truth is. Knowing what truth is and what makes a thing true is important. It is likely those who don't really understand what truth is are more at risk of being deceived than those who do understand what truth is.

One of the objects in serious discourse about philosophy, politics, business solutions, family matters is to reach agreement about the way a thing is in reality or about the best solution to a problem. This usually involves discovering the *truth* about something or discerning the *truth* or falsehood of a statement or representation.

The tools of discourse and precepts of dialogue are all about truth, or should be. In communicating our thoughts, desires, feelings, ideas, needs and other things we want to give the person or persons to whom we are talking or writing a true picture of what we want, of what we are thinking, of an idea we have or of how we are feeling. In describing a situation or a philosophical concept, we want to be able to convey an accurate description. That is to say, we want to get at the *truth* of the matter.

There are many theories on what truth is and what makes a thing true. They can be found in any good encyclopedia on philosophy and on the Internet. But there is only one theory that is valid or true. And that is the correspondence theory or concept of truth. As we have seen everybody has pretty much the same subconscious concept of what truth is and it is the correspondence concept. And everybody, or nearly everybody, bases their actions on this subconscious view.

The definition of truth, according to the Correspondence Theory of Truth, is:

Truth is the correct representation of the way a thing is in reality.

For example, we see a black cat. We have that image in our mind and we say, "There is a black cat." The image in our mind corresponds to the black cat, which exists outside our mind. We can say the image is true and the statement is true. The one exists in objective reality, the other exists in subjective reality. Thus we can also define truth as the correspondence of subjective reality with objective reality.

Everyone subconsciously accepts this. You accuse someone
of something that he didn't do and he will say, "that is not
true." You give someone five ones for a five-dollar bill and
say, "I gave you the correct change." And he will say, "That
is true."

But consciously it is another story. Ask 100 people to define
truth and you will get many different answers. Strangely, it is
rare that anyone will take the time to look up the definition in
a dictionary. In informal interviews of several hundred
people, close to half of those interviewed voiced the opinion
that truth was relative. That is that truth depended on each
person's perception. Only two or three percent were able to
articulate a correct philosophical definition of truth. A large
number said truth was what the Bible says. In reality, what
the Bible says does not make a thing true. What makes a
thing true is whether a statement corresponds to the way a
thing is in reality. This applies to what the Bible says or any
statement from any source for that matter.[3]

IF TRUTH WERE RELATIVE

If truth were relative, there could be no moral standards.
Lying, cheating, stealing, even killing, could be justified
from the viewpoint of certain individuals. For the most part,
people's *subconscious* understanding of what is truth is not
relative. It is based on objective reality and the perception of
that objective reality is the same for everybody. There is an
objective standard that everybody unconsciously accepts.
People who make the truth dependent on their viewpoint, that
is relative to them, are not being honest with themselves.
They are making truth the way they want it to be and thereby
divorcing it from objective reality. If a person is seriously out
of touch with objective reality, he is said to be neurotic.
Granted, there is an element of inexactness in the way we
perceive external reality. But inexactness is different from
relative.

A word needs to be said about the right of a person advancing a position to define the terms and concepts he uses in advancing a position (Precepts VI and VII). We will maintain that this right is not absolute in that there is at least one major exception. And that is the definition of truth. For *meaningful communication* to be meaningful, it is necessary that there be only one definition of truth, namely the correspondence theory of truth. This does not preclude the debating of other theories of truth. It does preclude the use of other theories of truth in advancing different positions.

We have said that a thing that exists in objective reality can also exist as a perception in subjective reality in the mind. What we are talking about is perception. That is.. it is not the thing itself that exists in the mind, but a perception of that thing or its representation in the mind. In a sense it goes through a process of conversion so it is a meaningful representation to the person perceiving it. This is the case of the perception of color and sound. The mind converts electromagnetic waves in objective reality into corresponding colors of objects; and sound waves in objective reality into corresponding sounds. And we now have instruments so that we can better understand what these different waves that we perceive as sights and sounds look like in objective reality. How we perceive them, classify them and reduce them into images, concepts and terms is the subject of Chapter VI.

Many *great* philosophers have expounded on what truth is and what makes a thing true.[4]

A NEGATIVE UNIVERSAL STATEMENT GENERALLY CANNOT BE PROVEN BUT IT CAN BE DISPROVED

CHAPTER V
THE NATURE OF PROOF

The purpose of proof is to determine what to believe and what not to believe. Understanding how the nature of proof fits into the scheme of things will aid in the determination of what to believe and what not to believe and to come to productive conclusions in constructive dialogue.

There are probably very few, if any, students majoring in philosophy who have not heard a professor say "You cannot prove" this or that. One of the more common statements is "You cannot prove the existence of external reality," or something to that effect. What is left unsaid is: You cannot prove that you cannot prove the existence of external reality.

Generally speaking, as proffered in Chapter I, a negative universal cannot be proven. It can be disproved, but not proven. Many, probably most, negative particular propositions cannot be proven. They can be disproved by proving the existence of facts that contradict the negative proposition.

The statement "You cannot prove that 'P'" in which "P" is a proposition, either particular or universal, also cannot be proven. In other words, you cannot prove that you cannot prove something. This is reminiscent of the statement, "All general statements are false, including this one." There is a truth expressed in these statements in that general statements tend to be false and propositions that "You cannot prove that 'P'" tend to be such that they cannot be proven. Likewise other negative statements tend to be such that they cannot be proven.

THE NATURE OF PROOF

Just what is proof and of what does it consist? It is likely we have all been confronted at one time or another with the challenge of "prove it!" How do we prove something and more importantly to whom do we "prove it!"

There are many ramifications to these questions, which are not immediately obvious. One of these ramifications is that statements which claim that this or that proves this or that may be false in that they prove no such thing. As we have seen statements that this or that proves a negative proposition is very likely to be a false claim.

Statements that this or that proves a proposition are based either on conclusions drawn from a priori premises (deductive reasoning) or empirical evidence. In all cases of a priori reasoning, conclusions are true if the premises are true and the argument is valid. Whether the premises are true is often determined by empirical evidence. Empirical evidence rests either on scientific facts or, as in law, on the rules of evidence which have long been debated in court proceedings. The validity of an argument is determined by the rules of logic.

Another ramification is the epistemological problem of justification, which brings up questions about knowledge and beliefs. To briefly summarize the problem, today's epistemologists generally hold there are three elements that are essential to the concept of knowledge.

They are truth, belief and justification. For knowledge to be knowledge it must be true, it must be believed and the one believing it, must be justified in doing so. The problem of justification is complicated and takes up a major portion of contemporary epistemology.[1]

For a person to be justified in his belief of a particular thing, he must have proved to himself that it is true. Our definition of proof (which is practical) is: *Anything at all that conclusively demonstrates that a thing is the way it is represented to be.* This is the concept of proof in the real world of common sense. It is slightly different from the concept of justification in the ephemeral world of epistemology.

Much of epistemology, if not nearly all, is speculative; that is there are almost as many opinions as there are epistemologists. Our approach here has to do with the practical application of philosophy to every day life. Not much practical application can be drawn from speculative philosophy. On the other hand there are many practical applications of basic axioms which are the ingredients of basic philosophy.

Here is an example of a thing that has been conclusively demonstrated to be true. There were people at certain periods of history who believed the earth to be flat. Science has demonstrated conclusively that the earth is round. The evidence is so conclusive that we all accept that (except members of the Flat Earth Society).

Which brings up the question of majority agreement involving particular positions. This used to be expressed as "counting cabbages" (heads), which does not determine whether a statement is true or false. However, the fact that there is disagreement on whether a particular statement is true or false, is not a determining factor either. In the academic climate of today there are very few positions in which there will not be one or more individuals holding an opposing viewpoint, especially on matters of philosophy.

And where there is a consensus on a particular theory or position held by a majority of professionals in a particular discipline, it may be a good indication (not proof) that that particular position is true, particularly if there is only a minor fringe element such as the Flat Earth Society in opposition.

Such is the case when we state there is conclusive proof the earth is round, it rotates on its axis and it revolves around the sun. We are totally justified in believing this based on scientific evidence.

We are also justified in believing the principles of mathematics, physics and other sciences and the basic principles of reality such as the principle of contradiction formulated by Aristotle in his Metaphysics.

There are those who will say these cannot be proved (a negative universal), which brings up the subject of "to whom" this or that can or cannot be proved. The "to whom" factor is at the heart of what the nature of proof consists. The "to whom" factor has three applications. They are individual, communal and theoretical. The first two have to do with the practical world of common sense. The third has to do with the esoteric world of theoretical knowledge. The first application is individual. It is up to each individual to decide what to believe or not to believe, what to accept into his belief system or exclude from his belief system.

As stated before, a belief system is the totality of beliefs of a philosophy, a religion or an individual. In regard to the individual it is the sum total of what he consciously believes to be true. In this sense proof that a thing is true or false consists in what each individual is justified in believing. Each individual must justify (prove) to himself that such and such is true.

The second application involves demonstrating to one or more other people that a thing is the way it is represented to be. Thus this application of proof revolves around assistance or persuasion, because we cannot force another person or group of people to accept our proof of something.

Fortunately, in philosophical discourse, there are rules for doing this, which makes one's position and/or arguments or "proof" subject to objective review. Traditionally, these include the principles and rules of logic and metaphysics. It is through observance of these principles and rules that we can justify to ourselves and others that our premises are true and that our arguments are valid.

There are those who, no matter how convincing the evidence, will not accept a thing to be true or false. People in this category are termed logically invincible. A person who rigidly maintains a position despite conclusive evidence to the contrary commits the fallacy of invincible ignorance. A person who is logically invincible is not a good subject with whom to engage in meaningful communication.

The third application of "to whom" is more often to nobody and consists of professional theorizers (generally university professors or scientists) making the case of why a certain position or theory is correct or incorrect, or best explains something. This third option is characterized by a number of philosophers as proving something to the universe.

Thus in light of this review of the nature of proof, many statements that purport to prove something or make a case for something do no such thing. It is an old philosophical adage that when approaching certain subjects, we maintain a "healthy scepticism." When we do, we are more likely to spot statements that falsely purport to prove something. This is particularly true in regard to negative statements. All this is relevant to constructive dialogue in which two or more people pursue resolutions to disputed questions.

CHAPTER VI
THE USE OF LANGUAGE

Much of philosophy of the last century was concerned with the analysis of language. Much of this study of language was concerned with the use of words and to an extent with the relation of words with concepts. There was debate over the existence of "universals." There were some who doubted the relevance of universal concepts and to some extent the nature of the distinction between external reality (everything outside the mind) and internal reality (everything inside the mind), though it may not have been couched in those terms. Without this distinction, definitions are devalued and class distinctions are blurred.

As noted in the Foreword of this book, there are people—even highly educated people—who are at fault in communicating because they use terms with which other people are unfamiliar. A rich vocabulary is to be admired. Even in simple everyday discourse we use terms that other people do not understand and other people use terms we do not understand. It makes us appear erudite. This probably occurs more often then we think. There is even a common expression for it. We, or they, are said to be "talking over their, or our, heads." Of course this also refers to argumentation and logic such as when one is arguing beside the point. Still in both instances the root cause is often lack of people having the same, or even any, understanding of the meaning of certain terms being used. We just don't know the extent of another person's vocabulary.

There are different tacks we can take from here. We can take up the whole theory of language as developed by a whole string of philosophers. This clearly is beyond the scope of this book, let alone this chapter. Or we can simplify matters by dealing with how written and spoken words communicate meaning from one person to one or more other persons. That is we can look into how words create data in the mind.

MEANINGFUL COMMUNICATION

Meaningful communication involves sending and receiving information in the form of verbal or written words. For words to be meaningful they must represent something in the mind such as images, ideas and concepts. These images, ideas and concepts are communicated by means of terms. Terms consist of one or more words. For terms to have meaning they must represent precisely the same thing to the person using them as to the person or persons receiving them. That is, they must represent the same concept to each person involved in dialogue. Therefore, they must be explained or defined so that every person involved in *meaningful communication* has the same understanding of what is meant.

Most terms used in every day speech have a generally accepted meaning to the people using them. But often, even in every day speech, one or more terms will be misunderstood by one or more people communicating with each other. In philosophical dialogue and in technical and legal matters this is a major problem. To avoid this, definitions are employed.

The terms we use exist both in external reality and internal reality. In external reality these terms consist of words or symbols on paper or sounds if we speak them. These words written or spoken also exist as an exact copy in internal reality—the mind.

Terms in the mind exist in two forms, an image of how they appear in external reality and either an image or concept for what they represent.[1] Thus we can define image as a concrete representation of an object in external reality such as that individual person named Harry or that certain Ford car with a dent in the fender. The image evoked in the mind is a picture of the Ford and the picture of the term.

CONCEPT OF A CONCEPT

We can define concept as an abstract piece of *mind data* that per se exists only in internal reality. Thus we can abstract from the image of that particular Ford and form a concept of *carness*—encompassing all cars—or *Ford car*—all cars made by Ford Motor Company—and apply these two concepts to each individual car or each individual car made by Ford Motor Company. But in another sense a concept may also exist in external reality in the form of a term by which we communicate what we mean when we write or speak the word car or Ford (car). This term, in turn, is represented in the mind as a concrete image by which the abstract concept is given meaning.

Now here is where it gets a little complicated and philosophers have gone off in all different directions to explain how it works.

We will keep it simple and obvious. There are two parts of an abstract concept as it exists in the mind. The abstract part of it does not per se exist in external reality, but the term we use to describe the abstract part exists in both internal reality and external reality in the form of the term we use to communicate it.

There are those who say the ideas of "courage" or "beauty" have existence outside the mind as Plato held. We won't argue that point here except to note that it would be interesting to know the place where they reside outside someone's mind. We won't be drawn into a discussion of all the positions held by certain philosophers, which may result from failure to recognize or confusion about the distinction between external and internal reality.

We can understand how the term of "courage" or "beauty" exists outside the mind but not the concept itself which we can apply to different aspects of it in external reality. Technically speaking, we can only form a new concept through descriptions or definitions of it. We can also learn a new concept by experience over time by how other people use the term of "courage" or "beauty."

An idea is similar to, or the same as, a "concept," depending on how it is used. We will distinguish the two by saying a concept is usually represented by a single term while an idea can be represented by a single term or many terms.

For proof or justification of this explanation, we can conjure up illogical "terms" that are only words and don't exist in the mind except as words. Take the words "square circle." We can say or write the words "square circle." But "square circle" is not a term because we cannot conceive of how a "square circle" looks and we cannot draw a "square circle." It is just two words spoken or written, that really have no representation in external reality.

This is all very elementary and we will not be led beyond it. This is all we need to delve further into the "Ten Precepts of Dialogue," and "Meaningful Communication," which is our mission here.

Great thinkers do not necessarily need words or terms to create great thoughts. They only need words or terms in communicating those great thoughts to others in the outside world. Thus we are in conflict with those who reduce philosophy to language in that we are reducing language to a secondary role of communicating thoughts—the ideas and concepts—that great thinkers, or anyone else, has produced. In our position, language—words and terms—are secondary while ideas and concepts are primary.

All images, concepts, ideas—all thoughts—are a part of subjective reality. They may not exist in the real world or in objective reality. In a practical sense, only an image in the mind exists as its object outside the mind. In an abstract sense, symbols on paper or other media, may represent in the external world abstract concepts that exist in the mind.

In other words, particular things which images represent exist in objective reality as do things that can't be seen or touched or that have no mass which are represented by concepts. Examples of things in objective reality that are represented by concepts are electricity, atoms and sub-atomic particles. They are represented by concepts because we do not have images of them. We only have images of the words written or spoken by which we communicate concepts. And it is a reasonable assumption that only a tiny part of objective or external reality is perceived by men and thus is represented in the collective mind of man.

It is important to note that the same image or concept may be conjured up in different ways with different words making up different terms. Thus two philosophers might be in disagreement about a position because of the terms they use and/or the description they employ. In effect they might hold the same position (exemplified by the same concept), but use different terms to describe it. The disagreement may be resolved by distinguishing and defining descriptions and terms. Preliminary analysis of responses by philosophers in polling on the concept of truth indicate this is the case to at least some degree involving the various theories being proffered about what truth is.

The problem of universals, in which there is currently a great deal of debate, is another instance in which different terms may be used to apply to the same concepts. The way the term "identity" is employed by different philosophers is an example of the way the same term may be used to apply to different concepts.[2]

These issues may play a part in the debate on the analysis of language which has resulted in many competing theories over the past century. And they are highly relevant to communication, especially philosophical dialogue. When "the sole concern of philosophical analysis is to root out the *source* of philosophical confusion," which is "the confused use of language," namely words, the importance of people's perception of how universal concepts are formed is evident.[3] This is what happened when the meaning of words are changed. Wittgenstein called it *word games* and these *word games* have pervaded popular culture. So in dialogue one must be aware of *word games*.

This is what Malcom Muggeridge saw when he said:

> ...one of the things that appals me and saddens me about the world today is the condition of words. Words can be polluted even more dramatically and drastically than rivers and land and sea. There has been a terrible destruction of words in our time.

> ...if we lose the meaning of words, it is far more serious in practice than losing our wealth or our power. Without our words, we are helpless and defenceless; their misuse is our undoing.[4]

CHAPTER VII
BELIEF SYSTEMS

A brief word about belief systems is relevant here. Everybody has a conscious belief system and at least one subconscious belief system. A belief system is the sum total of all beliefs held by a person or within the parameters of a particular theory, position or entity such as an explanation of a phenomenon, a philosophy, a religion or a sect. It is likely that most, if not all, personal, philosophical and religious belief systems contain certain beliefs that are false.

In meaningful communication the belief systems of the people involved may need to be taken into account because certain beliefs tend to be an obstacle to meaningful communication. In many, if not most, instances beliefs that are obstacles are based on prejudgments of other people or things and are made on the basis of some emotion such as fear, greed, anger, envy or jealousy. We call these beliefs prejudices. Quite often they are the result of ethnical, familial and social groupings, and even educational disciplines. Even philosophy professors are not immune. In fact psychiatrists (at least one and probably many, if not most, who are versed in philosophy) believe that a philosopher's perception of reality—which includes errors in his belief system—is what shapes his philosophy. There are different terms used by psychologists for belief system, but they generally refer to the same concept.

In reviewing the *Way Things Are* series with people, many have become angry at the definition of truth, the results of surveys asking people their definition of truth and at the Precepts of Dialogue. They have a fear of being hemmed in. Confronted with it, a prominent attorney said, "I hate to be setup to be proven wrong and stupid." Another person, a counselor, said, "I don't believe in definitions and I don't need rules to communicate." This particular counselor was highly educated in a number of subjects and had two Ph.Ds.

These people were adamant and refused to even engage in meaningful communication. It was impossible to talk to them about certain ideas and concepts. A number of academics have responded in the same way. One, a philosophy professor, indicated he did not believe a person had a right to certain positions or a right to define terms for use in explaining those positions. He objected to a definition used by a prominent author, a violation of the Sixth Precept.

INVINCIBLE IGNORANCE

There are people who do not believe two plus two always equals four. There are people who do not accept one or more of the first four principles of reality as stated in Chapter III. And there are people, as previously stated, who will not accept a fact no matter how convincing the proof. These people are logically invincible and it is impossible to engage in meaningful communication with them at least on certain subjects.

Being logically invincible is committing the fallacy of Invincible Ignorance. A fallacy is an argument, a form of reasoning, that on the surface appears valid, but upon further examination proves to be invalid. There are many kinds of fallacies. A brief introduction to fallacies is made in Chapter VIII.

It needs to be stated then that generally for meaningful communication to take place, there needs to be an element of trust generated between the participants. Many people are neurotic in this regard, perhaps because they are protecting beliefs in their belief system they unconsciously know are false.

Psychologists tell us we have two belief systems, one conscious and one subconscious. We often don't know what our subconscious beliefs are until we act on them or are unable to act because of them. They at times result in anti-social behavior. Uncovering these subconscious beliefs is a field of psychiatry popularized by Freud, Adler and Jung at the turn of the 20th Century.

So it needs to be understood that meaningful communication is a very special kind of communication and it can be and often is richly rewarding. People involved have to be open-minded and accept the ground rules.

The ultimate purpose of the precepts of dialogue is to arrive at the truth of any given matter and thereby enhance our understanding of the way things are. And the basic premise of this is that the truth cannot harm your belief system or you. But, as the Bible says, it can set you free.

This is a liberating concept—that the truth, the true perception of the way things are in reality—cannot harm you or be detrimental to your self image or your understanding of things. Realization of this is probably, or at least should be, the object, or at least one of the objects, of psychoanalysis or counseling. Psychologists may view this differently, but here again we may run up against the classic use of different words to refer to the same or similar objects or concepts.

MUCH OF THE INFORMATION

WE ARE DAILY CONFRONTED

WITH IS FALSE

CHAPTER VIII
DECEPTION

Much of the information we are daily confronted with is false. Discerning what is true from what is false is a function of philosophy. Philosophy provides certain tools to do this. We have discussed many of them in the previous chapters. A study of the fallacies provides us with additional tools. Knowledge of the fallacies enables us to spot an invalid argument and thereby discern what may be a false statement.

In the 5th and 4th Centuries B.C., when philosophy was reaching its zenith in Greece, there were itinerant teachers (philosophy professors) who developed clever arguments to sway their listeners to any point of view. They were looked down upon and disparaged by Socrates, Plato, Aristotle and other so-called reputable philosophers. Aristotle wrote a treatise on fallacies, *De Sophisticis Elenchis* (*On Sophistical Refutations*), to refute the arguments they used.

These itinerant teachers became known as "sophists," from which we derive the word sophism. A sophism is defined as a fallacious argument. A fallacious argument or fallacy is defined as an argument that at first appears to be valid, but upon closer examination turns out to be invalid.

To understand this we need to understand what an argument is and of what an argument consists. An argument is an inference. An inference is a conclusion drawn from one or more premises. A premise is a statement used in an argument from which a conclusion is drawn.

Premises and conclusions can be true or false. An argument is said not to be true or false, but valid or invalid, depending on whether or not the inference was correctly made. The truth or falsity of a conclusion is determined by the truth or falsity of the premises and by whether an argument is valid or invalid.

The rules of logic, which determine the validity of an argument, are too extensive to be treated here. And as stated before, one does not need to master them to spot an invalid argument. But one should be aware that they exist.

The fallacies provide us with examples of how these rules are violated as well as other ways we can be deceived. Textbooks on logic will usually list the different classifications and many examples. And there are many sites on the Internet that cover them.

One of the best sites on the Internet that covers the subject is http://www.fallacyfiles.org. It lists some 160 different kinds of fallacies and examples.

CHAPTER IX
TEN PRECEPTS OF DIALOGUE

Communication between two or more people is such an important factor in the quality of our lives that we all need to work on it. Few, if any, would argue there is no room for improvement. Communication takes effort. It's work. Here, in this chapter, are some constructive steps to take to make it work.

There are a number of terms that refer to different aspects of communication such as discourse, rhetoric, dialogue, dialectic, argument, debate, discussion, conversation. As stated previously, this book is about dialogue which we define as *constructive discourse between two or more people about a specific subject.*

Discourse is defined as *formal discussion of a subject.*

Rhetoric is defined as *the art or study of using language effectively and persuasively.*

Dialectic is defined as *the art or practice of arriving at the truth by the exchange of logical arguments.*

Argument has a number of definitions within the context of communication. The one we will use here is *a discussion of different points of view.* A logical argument is *the setting out of an inference by which a conclusion is drawn from one or more premises.*

Debate is defined as *a contest in which opposing sides defend and attack a position.* Further extensive exposition on the difference between debate and dialogue is in Chapter X.

Discussion is defined as *talking things over.*

Conversation is *an informal exchange of speech.*[1]

As stated in Chapter II and will be recounted in Chapter XI, there have been many writers who have listed and expounded on many rules and precepts of communication. They are nearly all helpful in furthering constructive dialogue and it is well to keep them all in mind. Here we will distinguish between the tools of discourse and the precepts of dialogue. The precepts of dialogue consist of rights and obligations. The tools of discourse encompass the precepts of dialogue, rules of civility or etiquette and good manners, and other helpful suggestions.

Of all these, the following Ten Precepts of Dialogue are especially powerful tools that can be used to enhance communication in general and dialogue in particular. What makes them powerful is how they can be used. This is discussed in the last chapter.

These precepts, while they are especially applicable to dialogue, apply to all the above forms of communication. It should be pointed out, as is explained below, that the use of the First Precept in dialogue and debate may vary from other forms of communication regarding the right to advance a false position or false statement.

This chapter lists and explains these Ten Precepts of Dialogue. They are:

1. Right to Position
2. Right to State and Define Position
3. Obligation to Receive Position
4. Right to Disagree
5. Right to Verify
6. Right to Define Terms
7. Obligation to Accept Terms
8. Obligation to distinguish position and person
9. Obligation to not impute
10. Obligation to Abide by Rules of Logic

There are some basic assumptions that need to be made in working with these precepts.

To paraphrase C. S. Lewis, we can learn something by listening to the kind of things people say. They say things like, "How would you like it if someone treated you that way... That is my seat, I was here first... Go to the end of the line... Give me a bit of your orange; I gave you a bit of mine... Come on, you promised... It is my turn to speak..."[2]

People who are saying these kind of things are appealing to a standard of behavior which they expect every other person to know about. The precepts are this kind of standard. They are the ten commandments of discourse. Everybody, or nearly everybody, will accept and use them when they are informed of them and educated in the use of them. For the individual who will not accept one or more of these precepts, this is the first issue to be resolved, hopefully by the process outlined herein, by *constructive dialogue*.

In all forms of verbal and written communication there is the person doing the talking and there is the person or persons doing the listening. To simplify discussion of the precepts, we will refer to the person doing the talking as the communicator. And we will refer to the person or persons doing the listening as the communicatee(s). As noted in Chapter V on proof, many philosophers speak of addressing a *universal* audience. The internet has made it possible to in effect have an interactive dialogue with a universal audience through a forum or other program.

The Ten Precepts of Dialogue are proffered as a means to keep everybody involved in dialogue on an equal footing. In an ideal world, there would be no need for the Ten Precepts of Dialogue. Like the Ten Commandments, they are there to guide human behavior. They are only of use when someone does not abide by them.

First we are dealing with a person advancing a position, who is the communicator. Secondly, we are dealing with the person or persons being addressed, the communicatee(s). Thirdly, we are dealing with everybody, communicator and communicatees alike.

I. Everybody has a right to his position, to advance it, to change it, to raise an issue, and to make and advance a true statement.

> This may not be as simple as it sounds. That everyone has a right to believe what he wants or decides to believe is a fundamental right recognized by law in democratic countries and by society. It is an adjunct of freedom of speech. It is also inherent in the moral responsibility that each person must take for his actions. If each person is responsible for his actions then he must have the right to govern those actions since his actions are governed by what he chooses to believe in.

This right is guaranteed its citizens by the First Amendment to the Constitution of the United States of America. It says:

> Congress shall make no law respecting an establishment of religion or prohibiting the free exercise thereof, or abridging the freedom of speech, or of the press; or the right of the people peaceably to assemble, and to petition the Government for a redress of grievances.

This right of freedom of speech has been upheld in many rulings by the U.S. Supreme Court. Even the right to put your money where your mouth is, so to speak. This means you have a right to believe what you want or decide to believe and advance your position in public.

A position is a particular belief or stand a person holds to. A particular belief or position can usually be summed up in a brief statement. And as such can be analyzed and debated. Thus a particular position can become an issue in meaningful communication. And each person has a right to his position and to change it.

This right is also implied in the term, "academic freedom." The U.S. Supreme Court has identified academic freedom as a right protected by the First Amendment, which guarantees freedom of speech.

Another affirmation of this right is the stand of the American Association of University Professors. According to the Statement of Principles of this association, "The common good depends on the free search for truth and its free exposition."

But does a person have a right to advance a position that is false, a common every-day occurrence in our society. It is done by people who are mistaken in their belief that a false position is true. And it is done by people who advance a position as true all the while knowing it to be false.

In discussing this right then, the question arises of representing to others as true something that is false. This is a moral question. To phrase it another way does a person have a right to lie? And of course, in the case of a grievous matter, the answer is no. So we must make the distinction of how this right is exercised.

We acknowledge that a person has a right to his position and the right to advance his position in public. We also acknowledge that a person does not have the right to deceive other people in ways that will harm other people or society.

How the right to a position is exercised then determines its validity. We will therefore make the distinction of the exercise of this right within and without the parameters of meaningful communication. We will hold that the right to hold a false position within the parameters of meaningful communication is valid. And the right to hold a false position outside the parameters of meaningful communication may be or may not be valid depending on circumstances.

In other words, here, we are concerned with the exercise of this right only as it applies to the precepts of dialogue. We acknowledge that this right exists beyond the extent of *meaningful communication*. To what extent, we are not concerned with here. Since we are not concerned here with the exercise of this right outside of meaningful communication, we will maintain it only as it applies to meaningful communication.

In formal debate, a person may defend a position he knows to be false. Outside of formal debate, a person may also take or hold a position he does not believe is true. In the teaching of philosophy, for example, many positions are advanced that are false. So, does one have the right to advance a false philosophy, knowing that it is false without identifying it as such?

And of course this "question" applies in all sorts of other areas such as advertising, politics, lawmaking and personal relations. It is a question we will take up at a later date and discuss in Book Nine of *The Way Things Are* series, *The Defamation of Truth*.

RIGHT TO CHANGE POSITION

And now we come to an additional right. And that is the right to change our position, at will, if you please. We are all in a search for truth or should be. If we can be shown the error of our ways we must change them. If we can be shown that a position we hold is false, we must change it. For many, if not most, depending on the position we are about to change, this moment can be a catharsis. It is something that could change our lives. This will be discussed further in the Tenth Precept where we deal with the commandment that we must accept what has been proven to be true and people who are logically invincible.

But, however the gravity, the right to change our position is inherent in our right to hold a position. Implied in this right is the obligation that a person committed to meaningful communication must be willing to change his position. We are not dealing with courtroom drama here. What we are talking about is a friendly exchange of ideas that can lead an individual to a new understanding of the truth of the way a thing is in reality.

In summary then, the right to hold a position involves the right to be heard. And the right to be heard means you have the right to raise an issue.

II. Any communicator of a position or statement has the right to state and define a position and the obligation to defend that position or statement(s) (provide proof of their truth or validity).

Generally speaking, whenever there is a right there is a corresponding obligation. The First Precept establishes the right to hold a position. The Second Precept imposes an obligation to define that position. In other words the communicator has the obligation to explain or elaborate on what his position consists and to give reasons why it is valid and submit to questioning.

This right and obligation is applied here to philosophical discourse and meaningful communication. This precept follows from the first precept and freedom of speech. If you want your position understood you have the obligation to make it understood. You have to state and define your position.

Where communication often breaks down, whether in informal talk or in meaningful communication, is when the one advancing a position does not make clear exactly what his position is. Sometimes a position is not clear to the one advancing it. It behooves the one advancing a position and the one or ones receiving it to question the other regarding his or their perception of it.

With certain exceptions, it is the fault of the communicator if his position is not understood. There will be instances when other people will not want to understand another's position whether from lack of patience or just a plain closed mind or even prejudice against a person advancing a position. In these instances, this is not the fault of the communicator. In these instances, there may not be much he can do. But if he has a willing audience, it is up to him to make himself understood.

There will be people who are communicating a position who will not accept this. They will be people who think their audience is not capable of understanding their esoteric positions. Or they will be people who think other people are not worthy of their pearls of wisdom. This attitude is a violation of this precept. In nearly all instances of a lack of understanding of another's position, it is because the person explaining it is not doing a good enough job in expressing himself. It is unlikely that one will find a person willing to engage in meaningful communication, who does not have the ability to understand any position or theory when it is properly explained.

III. The persons being communicated to (the communicatees) have the obligation to themselves, to the person making a statement or maintaining a position and to society to correctly understand and accept the statement or position being communicated.

Just as it is the obligation of the one communicating a position to make himself understood, it is the obligation of those receiving that communication to understand the position being communicated. Accepting a position as that of the person communicating it is a matter of acknowledgment and being fair minded. Agreement is not in question. If everyone has the right to his beliefs, everyone else has the obligation to acknowledge this.

All too often there are people who will not accept what they think is another person's position much less try to understand it. If you are sincere in your desire to engage in meaningful communication, you will accept the position of the person advancing it. You will then want to understand it and you do this by asking questions and making observations.

AGREEMENT NOT IN QUESTION

This does not mean you have to agree with the position being communicated. It just means you have to understand the communicator. It also means as a matter of courtesy that you should communicate back to the person advancing a position that you understand his position and that you accept it as his position. To do this you need to make sure that you really do understand his position by verifying it with him.

Everyone wants to be accepted. This is a basic desire of human beings. By assuring the one communicating a position that you understand and accept his position, you are in effect building a bridge of understanding with that person. You are, in a way, accepting him. This, in effect, creates a bond of friendship, which can produce an understanding much deeper than it otherwise would be and makes disagreements on positions much more palatable. The right to disagree is the Fourth Precept. How that should be handled is the subject of the Fourth Precept.

IV. Any person has a right to disagree with the position and/or statement of any other person and to question that person.

Particular beliefs or positions can usually be summed up in a brief statement and as such can be analyzed and debated. In meaningful communication this must be kept on an impersonal level.

On a personal level this right can hit pretty close to home. People, as a rule, do not like to have their individual beliefs questioned by other people. There is an emotional element in finding fault with another person's beliefs and a corresponding defensive stance taken.

NEED TO RISE ABOVE CONFLICT

There are disagreements in all areas of human endeavor and a lot of conflict as a result. Because of the emotional element and problematic conflict, we need to take special care in challenging a position on which we disagree. In effect we need to rise above conflict and exercise a certain amount of tact.

It may also be noted here that in meaningful communication a person has the right to hold a position he knows to be false for the sake of argument. The purpose is to test the premises and conclusions of the opposing argument.

We have seen in the explanation of the First Precept that the right to a position is limited by how it is exercised. Outside of meaningful communication this right does not always apply even though the right is generally granted on the basis of freedom of speech. However, a statement that is false and harmful to another person or organization can usually be challenged in a court of law.

In meaningful communication, the objective is to resolve conflict by reaching agreement either on the truth and validity of a position or on the points of disagreement. Observance of the following three precepts will facilitate the accomplishment of this objective.

V. The person maintaining a position has a right to verify that all his statements and his position are correctly understood.

This is one of the more important precepts and is not always obvious. If you are the one advancing a position, you will want to ascertain that your position is correctly understood. The usual way to do this is by asking questions.

If a person disagrees with your position, the first question you ask yourself is why. If you are firmly convinced of the logic and the truth of your position, the next question you ask is how could someone disagree with a position you know to be totally true. There must be something wrong. And then you come to the crux of what the Ten Precepts of Dialogue are all about. That is finding the answer. And that is what is rewarding, enlightening and enriching in this kind of discourse.

First you must identify the precise points of disagreement. To identify the points of disagreement entails a meeting of minds on what are the elements of the position held and the premises and conclusions that lead to the affirmation or disaffirmation of the position you are holding. So the first step is the verification of the other party's precise understanding of what is at issue which is based on a thorough understanding of the position in question.

THE NEXT STEP

Once this is accomplished, we can proceed to the next step, which is either agreement as to the validity and truth of the position held or to the precise points of disagreement. If there is agreement, then the final objective of meaningful communication is accomplished in regard to that position. If there is disagreement, the further step is then to identify, distinguish and define the points of disagreement. Once the points are separated and defined, each one can then be analyzed and subjected to the tools of logic to determine its truth and validity. And this is continued until there is agreement on all points of disagreement.

To reach agreement, the originator of a position may need to go to extraordinary lengths to make sure his position is understood. That is why, he has the right to establish the terms he is using to explain his position. This is covered in the next chapter on the Sixth Precept.

VI. The person maintaining a position has the obligation and the right to distinguish and define (within the rules of logic) the terms and concepts he uses.

This is different from the first precept. The First Precept has to do with defining or explaining a position. This Sixth Precept has to do with defining or explaining a concept.

This precept has major implications. We do not know what the other person knows or does not know, so we must take into account the level of intellection (knowledge) that the person or persons we are talking to has. If the dialogue we are having is with one or two other people, the fifth precept comes into play in which we are able to question their understanding of the position advocated. If we are not sure about another person's knowledge, we can verify his or her understanding by asking questions. In the case of a group, this is not practical. Therefore, it never hurts to assume that we need to provide elementary explanations because if we are talking to a group or addressing the universe, what seems simple to the communicator may be unknown or mean something else entirely to the communicatees.

MENCEPT IS A NEW TERM[3]

As we have seen in Chapter VI, meaningful communication involves sending and receiving information in the form of *mencepts* or mind data, which are represented by terms. Often these *mencepts*, especially in philosophical discourse, consist of highly abstract concepts. This is often the case when a person is proposing a new theory or idea or position. And if a person has a right to his position, he not only has the right to make his position understood, but also the obligation to do so, if he is sincere.

The only way to create a new abstract concept is by definition and elaboration of that definition. In other words, the person advancing a new position does so by explaining what he means and this may even involve coining a new term or terms. Or it may involve using a traditional term in a new sense. Many of the terms used in computer science fit in this category. As we have seen in Chapter VI, there is much confusion on the use of words, terms and language.

There are those who will argue that you do not have the right to define the terms you use in advancing a position. They may disagree with your definition and therefore not accept it. This attitude is the result of a failure to recognize and accept the Principle of the Great Distinction. That is they fail to recognize the distinction of the way things are in the mind and the spoken or written expression of the way things are in the mind. They fail to recognize how abstract concepts are communicated. They fail to recognize that for abstract concepts to be communicated they must be defined or explained. Failure to recognize this is an out-of-hand rejection of their explanation and this results in an inability to receive the concept being communicated, and so raises an insurmountable obstacle to meaningful communication.

There is one major exception to this right. As we have explained in Chapter IV, this right does not apply to the definition of truth. The definition of truth according to the correspondence concept must be adhered to for meaningful communication to be meaningful. There are all kinds of deception that can result by changing the definition of truth.

Another example of the establishment of this right is the way laws are written. In most instances, in the United States when the Congress, a state legislature or other political entity creates a new law, a part of that law is a definition of terms.

There has been much written on definitions of terms. The subject is a subdivision of logic. There are many kinds of definitions and there are many rules for creating definitions. They can be found in many, if not most, text books on logic. They will also be discussed in Book Eleven in *The Way Things Are* series, *A Layman's Guide to Logic*.

VII. All those involved in dialogue have the obligation to accept and use the terms and concepts as defined by the person advancing a position.

This may not be obvious and is easily violated.

This applies to meaningful communication in the discussion of a particular position.

This is also one of the more important precepts and follows from the Sixth Precept. In fact, as stated in the previous precept, there will be many who will disagree with it. They may even argue against a position based on their definition of a term, which will be different than that of the person using it to explain his position.

You don't have the right to disagree with a definition of a term used by the person advancing a position. You have the obligation to understand his position. This is critical in many arguments. Often opposing sides in an argument are basing their support or opposition on different concepts they have of one or more terms being used. Simply put, if you are to understand another person's position, you must understand his explanation of it. To understand his explanation of it, you must understand and accept the terms he is using to explain it.

There are adherents who hold that terms are merely arbitrary and artificial symbols that we attach to things and have no relation to the way things are in reality. This is directly opposed to the Principle of the Great Distinction and the correspondence theory of truth. Therefore, this is a false philosophy.

There are many such false philosophies. To know this, we do not have to know which is false and which is not. We can conclude from the Principle of Contradiction that two philosophical belief systems that disagree with each other cannot both be true representations of the way things are in reality. Most of philosophy consists of positions that do not agree with each other. So we can conclude that many, if not most philosophical positions are false. Which is true and which is false is not relevant to this conclusion. Based on the Principle of Contradiction we do not have to know which if any is true to reach this conclusion.

VIII. All parties have the obligation to distinguish between a person and the position of that person.

There is a very real tendency in people to attack a person holding a position they do not agree with. In fact this is a tactic often employed by politicians against their opponents. It is the classic ad hominem. That means you attack the person making the argument and not the position he is advancing. It is a fallacy of relevance. The dictionary defines ad hominem as attacking a persons character to avoid discussing the issues.

In meaningful communication, you never ever criticize the person, you criticize the position of that person. Many people have known persecution; people attacking other people because of their beliefs. We can't make a difference in these instances of intolerance. We can make a difference in the way we communicate and engage in meaningful communication.

IX. All parties have the obligation to not impute to another person beliefs, knowledge, ignorance, feelings, thoughts, intentions, positions or any other thing.

Imputing is one of the most common and glaring mistakes made in all kinds of communications between two or more people. There is a tendency to judge other people, what another person believes, what he has knowledge of, what he is ignorant of, his feelings, what he is thinking and what his intentions are. The fact is these kinds of judgments are likely to be wrong and are an obstacle to meaningful communication. There is no way that one person can know what is in another person's mind. So this precept requires us to accept what another person says about his position or any other thing. If a person wants to know, then the thing to do is ask.

This precept echoes the Bible's admonition do not judge lest you be judged. Everybody has the right not only to his position, but to his beliefs, feelings, thoughts, intentions, likes and dislikes. These are integral to each person and only the person to whom they belong knows what they are.

Every person's ideas, beliefs, feelings, likes and dislikes differ in some degree from every other person's, ideas, beliefs, feelings, likes and dislikes. Nobody has the right to tell another person what he (the other person) believes or what his feelings are or what his position is on any subject. Likewise another person's knowledge or ignorance is not a legitimate subject of speculation, except perhaps in an academic setting.

This raises the specter of assumed accusations in which one person judges another on the basis of their own beliefs without taking into account that another person might have a different belief and as a result a different response to a specific act. There are many examples of this.

X. All parties have the obligation to abide by certain principles of reality, the laws of thought and certain principles and rules of logic and identification of fallacies.

This precept entails a basic understanding of certain elements of philosophy. There are many principles of reality and axioms in philosophy in addition to those discussed in Chapters I and III. The principle of contradiction and its use in disproving a negative universal is probably the most applicable to dialogue.

In addition, there are laws of thought, and principles and rules of logic, all of which apply to meaningful communication. These include rules for defining terms, rules for forming syllogisms and the identification of fallacies. These rules and fallacies are extensive and for most people who master them, they involve a certain amount of formal education.

However we all possess a native ability to reason and identify false arguments. A person need not be versed in all these rules and fallacies to engage in meaningful communication. However, a person needs to understand that they exist and to acknowledge that they are valid when confronted with them.[4]

There are many more tools of discourse. These tools will be reviewed in the next chapter and a number of them will be combined into the eleventh precept, which will be discussed in Chapter XI.

CHAPTER X
SURVEY OF LITERATURE

There is another side to the enhancement of constructive dialogue other than the rights and obligations expressed in the precepts. And that is civility and other rules and suggestions for enhancing dialogue. Civility carries dialogue to heights it would not otherwise achieve. George Washington listed 110 rules of civility. They are mainly concerned with etiquette or good manners. All 110 are listed on National Public Radio's website.[1] A number of them are listed below.

One organization that focuses on dialogue as we define it is the National Coalition for Dialogue and Deliberation (NCDD). It can be found at www.thataway.org. It answers the question: "So what are dialogue and deliberation anyway?"

Dialogue is a process that allows people, usually in small groups, to share their perspectives and experiences with one another about difficult issues we tend to just debate about or avoid entirely. Issues like racial disparities, youth violence and gay marriage.

Dialogue is not about winning an argument or coming to an agreement, but about understanding and learning. Dialogue dispels stereotypes, builds trust and enables people to be open to perspectives that are very different from their own. Dialogue can, and often does, lead to both personal and collaborative action.

Deliberation is a closely related process with a different emphasis. Deliberation emphasizes the importance of examining options and trade-offs to make better decisions. Decisions about important public issues like health care and immigration are too often made through the use of power or coercion rather than a sound decision-making process that involves all parties and explores all options.

Dialogue and deliberation processes tend to use skilled facilitators and carefully constructed ground rules or agreements to ensure that all participants are heard and are treated as equals. Inclusion is a critical element of both dialogue and deliberation, as a variety of perspectives, backgrounds, and levels of influence enrich the discussion and validate the outcomes.

Dialogue often lays the groundwork for deliberation. The trust, mutual understanding and relationships that are built during dialogue enable participants to deliberate more effectively, and to make better decisions. For groups that want to move from talk to a decision or action, NCDD recommends starting with dialogue and encouraging deliberation after people have had the chance to share their personal experiences with the issue at hand.

Tom Atlee, who authors the Co-Intelligence Institute at the web site www.co-intelligence.org, takes the concept of dialogue beyond the level of constructive discourse. He says,

Not all communication is dialogue. Dialogue is shared exploration towards greater understanding, connection or possibility. Any communication that fits this definition, the Co-Intelligence Institute considers dialogue. Communication that doesn't fit this definition , we don't call dialogue.

Atlee goes on to say:

Dialogue can at times be truly magical, dissolving the boundaries between us and the world and opening up wellsprings of realization and resonant power. In those rare, deeply healing moments of dialogue in its most ideal form, we may experience the wholeness of who we are (beyond our isolated ego), listening and speaking to the wholeness of who we are (deep within and beyond the group around us). At those times it is almost as if wholeness is speaking and listening to itself though us, individually and collectively...

He further says:

The late quantum physicist David Bohm observed that both quantum mechanics and mystical traditions suggest that our beliefs shape the realities we evoke. He further postulated that thought is largely a collective phenomenon, made possible only through culture and communication. Human conversations arise out of and influence an ocean of cultural and transpersonal meanings in which we live our lives, and this process he called dialogue.

Most conversations, of course, lack the fluid, deeply connected quality suggested by this oceanic metaphor. They are more like ping-pong games, with participants hitting their very solid ideas and well-defended positions back and forth. Such conversations are properly called discussions. "Discussion," Bohm noted, derives from the same root word as "percussion" and "concussion," a root that connotes striking, shaking and hitting.

Dialogue, in contrast, involves joining our thinking and feeling into a shared pool of meaning which continually flows and evolves, carrying us all into new, deeper levels of understanding none of us could have foreseen. Through dialogue "a new kind of mind begins to come into being," observed Bohm, "based on the development of common meaning... People are no longer primarily in opposition, nor can they be said to be interacting, rather they are participating in this pool of common meaning, which is capable of constant development and change."

Atlee continues:

The more all participants are aware of the nature of dialogue and committed to bringing it about, the better the chance it will happen. Towards that end, the following comparison of dialogue and debate offers one of the most useful summaries of dialogue that we've seen. (It was adapted by the Study Circle Resource Center from a paper prepared by Shelley Berman, which in turn was based on discussions of the Dialogue Group of the Boston Chapter of Educators for Social Responsibility.)

Dialogue is collaborative: two or more sides work together toward common understanding. Debate is oppositional: two sides oppose each other and attempt to prove each other wrong. In dialogue, finding common ground is the goal. In debate, winning is the goal.

In dialogue, one listens to the other side(s) in order to understand, find meaning, and find agreement. In debate, one listens to the other side in order to find flaws and to counter its arguments.

Dialogue enlarges and possibly changes a participant's point of view. Debate affirms a participant's own point of view.

Dialogue reveals assumptions for reevaluation. Debate defends assumptions as truth.

Dialogue causes introspection on one's own position. Debate causes critique of the other position.

Dialogue opens the possibility of reaching a better solution than any of the original solutions. Debate defends one's own positions as the best solution and excludes other solutions. Dialogue creates an open-minded attitude: an openness to being wrong and an openness to change. Debate creates a closed-minded attitude, a determination to be right.

In dialogue, one submits one's best thinking, knowing that other people's reflections will help improve it rather than destroy it. In debate, one submits one's best thinking and defends it against challenge to show that it is right.

Dialogue calls for temporarily suspending one's beliefs. Debate calls for investing wholeheartedly in one's beliefs.

In dialogue, one searches for basic agreements. In debate, one searches for glaring differences.

In dialogue, one searches for strengths in the other positions. In debate, one searches for flaws and weaknesses in the other positions.

Dialogue involves a real concern for the other person and seeks to not alienate or offend. Debate involves a countering of the other position without focusing on feelings or relationship and often belittles or deprecates the other person.

Dialogue assumes that many people have pieces of the answer and that together they can put them into a workable solution. Debate assumes that there is a right answer and that someone has it.

Dialogue remains open-ended. Debate implies a conclusion.

A different set of rules were proposed in a book on argumentation.[2] They were listed as "Rules for Critical Discussion" and are:

1. Parties must not prevent each other from advancing or casting doubt on each others viewpoints.

2. Whoever advances a viewpoint is obliged to defend it if asked to do so.

3. An attack on a viewpoint must represent the viewpoint that has really been advanced by the protagonist.

4. A viewpoint may be defended or attacked only by advancing argumentation that is relevant to that viewpoint.

5. A person can be held responsible for the unstated premises he leaves implicit in his argument.

6. A viewpoint is regarded as conclusively defended only if the defense takes place by means of argumentation based on premises accepted by the other party, and it meets the requirements of Rule 8.

7. A viewpoint is regarded as conclusively defended only if the defense takes place by means of arguments in which an argumentation scheme is correctly applied.

8. A viewpoint is regarded as conclusively defended only if supported by a chain of argumentation meeting the requirements of rules 6 and 7 and if the unstated premises in the chain of argumentation are accepted by the other party.

9. A failed defense must result in the proponent withdrawing her thesis and a successful defense must result in the respondent withdrawing his doubt about the proponents thesis.

10. Formulations of questions and arguments must not be obscure, excessively vague, or confusingly ambiguous and must be interpreted as accurately as possible.

From all this we can make up a list of rules of civility. For starters, here is some from George Washington's list that could pertain to dialogue:

1. Every action done in company ought to be with some sign of respect to those that are present.

12. Shake not the head, feet, or legs; roll not the eyes; lift not one eyebrow higher than the other, wry not the mouth, and bedew no man's face with your spittle by approaching too near him when you speak.

19. Let your countenance be pleasant but in serious matters somewhat grave.

47. Mock not nor jest at any thing of importance. Break no jests that are sharp, biting, and if you deliver any thing witty and pleasant, abstain from laughing thereat yourself.

49. Use no reproachful language against any one; neither curse nor revile.

58. Let your conversation be without malice or envy, for 'tis a sign of a tractable and commendable nature, and in all causes of passion permit reason to govern.

64. Break not a jest where none take pleasure in mirth; laugh not aloud, nor at all without occasion; deride no man's misfortune though there seem to be some cause.

65. Speak not injurious words neither in jest nor earnest; scoff at none although they give occasion.

66. Be not forward but friendly and courteous, the first to salute, hear and answer; and be not pensive when it's a time to converse.

73. Think before you speak, pronounce not imperfectly, nor bring out your words too hastily, but orderly and distinctly.

74. When another speaks, be attentive yourself and disturb not the audience. If any hesitate in his words, help him not nor prompt him unless desired. Interrupt him not, nor answer him till his speech be ended.

89. Speak not evil of the absent, for it is unjust.

There are some rules or commandments of reason which, while not rights or obligations, can be helpful in arriving at the truth of any matter in dialogue.[3] They include:

Do not accept as true anything that has not been proven to be true.

Do not unreasonably disregard anything that has not been disproved.

Never argue about established facts. Established facts can be ascertained from reference materials on the Internet and in print.

Distinguish fact from opinion.

Distinguish between particular and universal statements.

Classify information according to source, whether it is gained from experience, reasoned to or communicated.

Prove or disprove essential facts through research, and evaluate unverified communicated information according to established facts, physical evidence, corroborating testimony, fallacious reasoning and logical conclusions.

Accept what is true.

Reject what is false.

Withhold judgment on everything else.

To resolve disagreements always distinguish and define positions and terms.

There are many more adages that need to be added here. They will have to wait for another time. Material in print and on the Internet will continue to be reviewed and may appear here in future editions.

CHAPTER XI
USING PRECEPTS AND RULES

There is a tremendous advantage to anyone who knows and is able to use the Ten Precepts of Dialogue. As seen in Chapter IX, the Ten Precepts are more involved with rights and obligations while other adages of constructive discourse are more involved with rules of civility and etiquette and helpful suggestions. Using the ten precepts will be taken up first and then the other rules and suggestions.

We have tested the precepts of dialogue and they really work if they are used correctly and skillfully. To really use them, they must be on the tip of the tongue. We have found that memorizing them to have them on the tip of the tongue in the real world is not always practicable. Therefore we have listed the Ten Precepts on the last page of this book, which may be torn out and kept at hand during *dialogue* with others.

As stated previously, in a perfect world we would have no need of the Ten Precepts of Dialogue. But this is not a perfect world and people who wish to engage in constructive philosophical discourse will likely at one time or another violate one or more of the Ten Precepts of Dialogue.

To be effective in dialogue, we need to walk and talk softly and not "carry a big stick." There may be times when pointing out a violation of one of the Ten Precepts is counter-productive. The Ten Precepts should not be used as a weapon, but as a means of furthering greater understanding of the subject under discussion.

Occasions will arise in which you can redirect a conversation in a constructive manner. This is what each of the ten precepts can do. Here are some suggestions:

The First Precept of Dialogue says: *Everybody has a right to his position, to advance it, to change it, to raise an issue, and to make and advance a true statement.* .

> Sometimes a person needs to be reminded that in constructive discourse you or they do have a right to make a statement or hold a position and so it does not hurt to remind him, her or them of that:

>> I have a right to my position just as you and everybody else does.

> This has the effect of creating good will in any attempt at dialogue. You can continue:

>> "I have a right and obligation to change my position so if you can show me where I am wrong, I will change it. Where am I wrong?"

> This has the effect of opening up opportunities of dialogue with the person or persons you are in dialogue with. Some people are in love with their position and would be unwilling to change it no matter what. So it does not hurt to ask:

Do you think there is a possibility that you could be mistaken?

The answer will either be yes or no but more likely something like this:

I am not mistaken.

Don't give up. Ask:

Would you at least consider the possibility?

There are no correct answers here. One can keep probing or start distinguishing and defining the terms being used and ultimately the position being maintained.

Outside the area of dialogue, the First Precept may be used effectively against a politician, a journalist or any public speaker who intentionally advances a false position or makes a false statement. You can say:

You are in violation of the First Precept and Second Precept. You have no right to say that (or hold that) (state what is false). If you are going to make that statement (hold that position) you have the obligation to show evidence that it is true.

The Second Precept of Dialogue says: *Any communicator of a position or statement has the right to state and define a position and the obligation to defend that position or statement(s) (provide proof of their truth or validity).*

It is obvious that if you have a right to make a statement, you have a right to state it and define it.

The important thing here is the obligation to defend your position or statement. In other words, if you are going to take a stand, you must have good reason for doing so. Don't make empty statements that you cannot back up and prove. If you haven't thought something through it is best to remain silent. Thus you can say:

> I have a right to state my position just as you have a right to state your position. My position is.
> (state your position).

Now give reasons why you think your position is valid or your statement is true.

Dialogue is often fast-paced, particularly where there is more than two participants and people are vying for the opportunity to express their opinions. In case someone tries to change the subject, you can say:

> I have a right to promote my position. Let's stick to the subject of my position.

Here someone might break in and say:

> What gives you that right?

And you can say:

> I am guaranteed that right by the second precept of dialogue.

And they will probably reply with a two-word expletive that has to do with male bovine fecal matter. Don't lose your cool. You have the high ground.

You can say:

It's a fact. You can look it up.

And that should settle the matter. If it doesn't, you can bring up the Third Precept.

The Third Precept of Dialogue says: *The persons being communicated to (the communicatees) have the obligation to themselves, to the person maintaining a position and to society to correctly understand and accept the position being communicated.*

So you can say:

You see, you are obligated to correctly understand my position. It is a right guaranteed to me and an obligation imposed on you by the Third Precept.

And so it goes. And if you do use the precepts as part of your dialogue, soften their touch by explaining what dialogue is all about.

Dialogue is about me gaining a better understanding of what you are saying. And it is about you gaining a better understanding of what I am saying. We after all are trying to arrive at a solution to this problem. We can make this conversation constructive or not. Do you want to gain a greater understanding of things or not? To make this conversation constructive, we have to abide by a certain standard. There are many precepts of dialogue which provide that standard.

Here, with this opening, or somewhere else in the conversation, you can explain the value of having a set of rules to go by and list and explain the ten precepts of dialogue. That should duly impress your audience, whoever they may be, and further your goal of constructive discourse.

The Fourth Precept of Dialogue says: *Any person has a right to disagree with the position of any other person and to question that person.*

So you can say:

> I am not asking you to agree with my position. The fourth precept of dialogue gives you the right to disagree with my position. And I have a right to disagree with your position. But first I need to understand what it is. But right now we are talking about my position. When you understand my position, we will deal with your objections, which you have a right to make, and to lay out your position. Now, you have a right to question me and I have a right to question you. Okay?

The Fifth Precept of Dialogue says: *The person maintaining a position has a right to verify that all his statements and his position are correctly understood.*

So you can say:

> So, now that I have laid out my position, it is important that I verify that you correctly understand my position. That is my right under the fifth precept. Okay?

The Sixth Precept of Dialogue says: *The person maintaining a position has the obligation and the right to distinguish and define (within the rules of logic) the terms and concepts he uses.*

So you can say:

> Now it is obvious you do not understand what I mean by (state the term that is not understood). You see, I have the right to define the terms and concepts I use. That is what the Sixth Precept of dialogue says.

The Seventh Precept of Dialogue says: *All those involved in dialogue have the obligation to accept and use the terms and concepts as defined by the person advancing a position.*

So you can say:

> And you must accept and use my definition of the terms and concepts I use. Okay?"

> Okay. But it is obvious you are a high pressure salesman.

The Eighth Precept of Dialogue says: *All parties have the obligation to distinguish between a person and the position of that person.*

The communicatee may say:

> You are an ex-con.

And you can say:

> So what has that got to do with my position,

The Ninth Precept of Dialogue says: *All parties have the obligation to not impute to another person beliefs, knowledge, ignorance, feelings, thoughts, intentions, positions or any other thing.*

The communicatee may say:

> Okay, but you believe in certain things that you have no knowledge of. You feel you have the right to put something over on me. Your intention is to destroy me.

And you can say:

> No, you are totally violating the Ninth Precept, which says, "you shall not impute." You don't know what I believe or how I feel. I have no intention to do any such thing. You see, you are imputing to me things that are not true. You have no right to do this. If you still wish to engage in constructive dialogue, there are certain rules you must obey. We have gotten off the track here. Let's stick to the discussion of ideas and not personalities. Okay?

There is another element that must be considered here about imputing. Imputing means verbally assigning an attribute to another person, such as knowledge, beliefs, feelings, intentions without justification. It does not mean that we should not evaluate what another person knows or does not know. In constructive dialogue it is a good idea to keep in mind another person's level of intellection or knowledge, what another person knows or does not know. In fact, it doesn't hurt to ask.

The Tenth Precept of Dialogue says: *All parties have the obligation to abide by certain principles of reality, the laws of thought and certain principles and rules of logic and identification of fallacies.*

The study of logic and the fallacies enhances our ability to spot illogical conclusions and fallacious reasoning. However we don't need a degree in philosophy to think critically. We all have a common sense of how to do this and to reason correctly.

As stated above there is a tremendous advantage to anyone who knows and is able to use the Ten Precepts of Dialogue. This is especially true of the Tenth Precept. The Tenth Precept is consistently violated in all areas of communication–in political statements; in reporting, especially broadcast journalism; in debate, and in dialogue. It is easy for someone to slip into a fallacy in advancing a position or making a statement. This is especially true of the fallacy of improper generalization. Many, if not most, generalizations are false. This is a violation of the Tenth Precept.

One can say:

> That particular general statement is false. Just one exception makes it false.

Anyone serious about dialogue should review the fallacies. Most books on logic and critical thinking contain them. Online an extensive review is at www.fallacyfiles.org.

In addition to fallacies, one should consider the use of the "negative universal," the principles and laws of contradiction, identity and excluded middle. For example, one can say:

That is a negative universal. You can't prove
that negative universal statement. Your
statement is a violation of the Tenth Precept.

You can't have it both ways. That violates the
law of contradiction and the Tenth Precept. A
statement cannot be true and false at the same
time.

The statement you just made has to be either
true or false. You have to defend it.

Extra terrestrial beings either exist or they do
not.

My statement says what it says. To say
otherwise violates the law of identity and the
Tenth Precept.

And so on. The Tenth Precept contains an almost
unlimited number of useful tools. The basic ones we
have discussed in preceding chapters.

Not as important, since one is not obligated to abide
by them, are rules of civility, commandments of
reason and other helpful suggestions to enhance
dialogue that were reviewed in the previous chapter.
Here an Eleventh Precept can be created under which
the more applicable of these can be listed.

- Every action done in company ought to be with some
  sign of respect to those that are present.

- Use no reproachful language against any one; neither
  curse nor revile.

- When another speaks, be attentive yourself and disturb not the audience.

- Search for strengths in the other positions.

- Search for basic agreements.

- Show real concern for the other person and try not to alienate or offend.

- Be open-minded, open to being wrong, open to change.

- Listen to the other side in order to understand, find meaning, and find agreement.

- Do not accept as true anything that has not been proven to be true.

- Do not unreasonably disregard anything that has not been disproved.

- Never argue about established facts. Established facts can be ascertained from reference materials on the Internet and in print.

- Distinguish fact from opinion.

- To resolve disagreements always distinguish and define positions and terms.

These suggestions listed under the Eleventh Precept hardly need elaboration. The collective sense of propriety, which many of these rules of civility evoke and which effectively reigned in outlandish behavior in the first half of the 20th Century, progressively diminished in the second half of that century. We need to be reminded of them. See Appendix D for future editions of this book and other books in *The Way Things Are* series.

APPENDIX A
EPILOGUE

There is a tendency in academia to judge philosophical dissertation by the credentials of the one who wrote it, rather than the quality of what is written. Thus one never sees (or at least rarely sees) a paper, a position or an argument in instructional material that is not written by a PhD.

This is unfortunate because it is not who says it that matters. It is the substance of what is said that matters. We are often prejudiced in dismissing a statement by someone we consider unqualified.

This is an example of an argumentum ad hominem. One attacks the man rather than addressing the substance of an argument, statement or position.

In compiling the various treatises or books in *The Way Things Are* series, it is hoped that one will judge the quality of the contribution of the subject matter, rather than the credentials of the one who wrote it. This is what the Ten Precepts of Dialogue is all about. Hopefully in each book in the series a dialogue will take place according to the rules laid out in the ten precepts. Thus everyone is invited to take part, whether undergraduate, graduate or other.

Once a book is published, does not mean the end of the of
compilation of the text. Rather it is the beginning.
Everything can be improved upon. And the text of the
original publication should be looked upon as an outline for
future elaboration. And the first edition should be the
beginning of many future editions. As stated elsewhere, a list
of the contemplated books in the series is in Appendix D.

The purpose of the series and the object of philosophical
inquiry should be the discernment of truth about the subject
matter and the various positions related to that subject matter.

PLEASE NOTE: *These End Notes are posted online at*

www.wikiwacky.net/book02/appendixb.htm

You may access directly other websites listed in these End Notes by going to the above URL. Once there click on the chapter number at the top of the page. This will take you to all the End Notes in that chapter. You may then go directly to a referenced web site simply by clicking on the URL of that web site. which is in blue.

APPENDIX B
END NOTES

Foreword

1. This quote was taken from a brochure entitled *How To Release The Hidden Power Of Your Mind.* The brochure consisted of the text of Adler's speech which he gave to members of the "Million-Dollar Round Table," and a brief "Foreword" introducing Adler by "James B. Irvine, Jr., CLU, Chairman, 1961 Million Dollar Round Table." No other information about the brochure was given. Adler indicated in his speech that his position at the time was "Director of the Institute for Philosophical Research in San Francisco."

2. Wikipedia has a good biography on Adler. See also: http://www.nndb.com/people/593/000089326/

110

Preface

1. This is evident from the high degree of specialization each of these disciplines has reached and the profusion of esoteric terms each has produced. It is also evidenced within the philosophical community as is pointed out in Chapter VI on Language. Will Rogers is reported to have said, "Everyone is ignorant only on different subjects." And "There is no man as ignorant as an educated man when you get him off his subject."

Chapter:

III. The Role of Philosophy

1. This was said on Coast to Coast a.m. (Nov. 10, 2003) a popular radio talk show that was hosted by Art Bell that was broadcast over a large network of radio stations from 1 a.m. to 5 a.m. Eastern Time. Sometime after the above date, Art Bell resigned as host of the show on weeknights and his place was taken over by George Noory.

2. LePore, J. (2009). *A World I Never Made*, Kindle edition. Stamford, CT: The Aronica-Miller Publishing Project, LLC .

3. There are many examples of remarks similar to those above throughout literature. If you make the Great Distinction (between exterior and interior reality), it becomes obvious that our belief systems do not create reality. A person's belief system does, however, often determine the way a person perceives things (reality). Here again is the classic confusion between truth and perception and the failure to make the distinction between interior and external reality.

4. The term ideaism would be a more accurate label of the position of idealism.

5. The American Philosophical Association website is at http://www.apaonline.org/default.aspx   The Philosophical Documentation Center is at http://www.pdcnet.org/pages/ Products/directories.htm.   The APA website as of this writing (2011) listed a broad range of statistics on salary and benefits of philosophy professors. It was at: http://www.aaup .org/NR/rdonlyres/71558CEE-48B3-4AC7-AED8-0DD A86870C50/0/alltabs.pdf.

6. In regard to polling many professors and graduate students avoid taking a position or even addressing this issue, which makes it extremely difficult to make an accurate assessment on the percentage holding as valid any given position. Thus it must be understood that the listing of the results of a poll of philosophers is only an approximation.

7. About reporting is further discussed in Appendix D.

8. Most philosophers will agree that there is a distinction between external and internal reality. But this distinction can get overlooked in resolving conflicts between a number of opposing positions. The term, "the great distinction," was first used in Book I of They Way Things Are series. Hoppins, C. (1993), *Basic Precepts of Reality and Common Sense*, Boise ID: Western Research Press.

9. Schoedinger, A. B.(2000*) Our Philosophical Heritage*, Third Edition, Dubuque, Iowa: Kendall/Hunt Publishing Company, 482.

10. Saikat Guha, while an undergraduate student at Boise State University, was referring to Wittgenstein among others when he made an offhand remark, "...they don't understand the use of words."

11. Russell, B.A.W. (1912) Chapter 15, *The Problems of Philosophy*, Oxford University Press.

12. The principle of contradiction in the last half of the 20th Century became the principle of non-contradiction.

13. Polling indicates these principles have lost the significance they once held. For example there is a great deal of confusion regarding the principle of identity. Many confuse the principle of identity with the law of identity. At this writing the Cambridge Dictionary of Philosophy among others do not even list the principle of identity as a separate subject. It is however listed under the three laws of thought. Many philosophers do not make the distinction between the principles of identity, contradiction and excluded middle and the corresponding laws of thought.

14. See also principle of bivalence. Some philosophers make a distinction between the two.

IV. The Role of Truth

1. This list was taken from Wikipedia and The Stanford Encyclopedia of Philosophy. To entertain all these different positions is not within the scope of this book. At this writing, this current extensive review of the subject by Wikipedia can be found at http://en.wikipedia.org/wiki /Truth. Explanations of what truth is can also be found at the Stanford Encyclopedia of Philosophy at http://plato.stanford.edu/search/searcher.py?query=truth One paper on the subject is displayed in Endnote #4 below.

Please note you can click on all the links in these end notes and go directly to the referenced web sites by going to www.wikiwacky.net/book02/ appendixb.htm and clicking on the chapter number at the top of the page

2. There appears to be a lot of confusion in the answers to surveys among professional philosophers about the conflicting theories of what truth is. Preliminary analysis indicates that the overwhelming majority of professors and graduate students surveyed have the same or similar conception of the nature of truth. While labels differ, the explanations behind the labels are not all that incompatible with the correspondence theory of what truth is.

3. This poll has a long history. At first the results were not recorded. When it became evident that nearly every answer was different, we began recording the answers. Still it was very informal until 2010, when the results of it became an important element in this book and we realized that this was a very difficult question for people to answer and further questioning was usually needed to determine people's true perception of what truth is. For example a woman who held a master's degree in education from Harvard University said in answer to the poll in 2007, "Truth has always perplexed me. When I discuss this with people, they always have their own version. I am honestly unclear about what truth is."

A long list of other answers to the poll was on the Western Research website. As of this writing it could be accessed by going to www.wrii.org/.

At the beginning of 2011, we added the question "What makes a thing or statement true?" and set up a web site whereby we could classify the respondents as to gender, age, occupation and education level. As of this writing this web site was at www.irsonline.org. This web site is no longer taking responses. A person interested in providing their definition of truth may state it in an email to westernresearch@earthlink..net

4. The following excerpt on truth was written by Saikat Guha. It was excerpted from a paper entitled "The One: A Defense of Monism." It can be found along with the rest of Guha's published writings at www.saikatguha.com.

[The "truth-maker principle"] enjoys wide-spread acceptance among contemporary philosophers and seems fairly self-evident... It says that what is true is determined by what there is. In other words, truth supervenes on reality; what exists determines what the world is like, or which truths obtain. This is sometimes put by saying that every truth must have a truth-maker, something which, by existing, makes that truth obtain or be the case. A truth may have several truth-makers, which jointly support that truth (by all existing together), but it must have at least one. A more precise formulation of this principle may be made by reflecting that, for each existing thing, there is the truth, about that thing, that it exists. Thus, assuming that I exist, there is a truth about me which states my existence, and there is another for you, another for Lyndon Johnson, and so on. Let us call these particular existential truths. (We should understand these as the sort of truths that are expressed by singular existential sentences featuring proper names, like "Socrates exists". Of course we do not need to have proper names for all objects, or to know that they exist, in order for the relevant truths to obtain—they just have to exist.) Then there is a further truth which says, of all things taken together, that *these* are all the things that exist (that is, there are no other things besides these). This truth, together with the particular existential truths, are what we may call the *basic existential truths*. Then the truth-maker principle states that the basic existential truths jointly entail all truths. In other words, each and every truth supervenes on the basic existential truths, taken together. This formulation avoids a problem of the earlier version: we need not be puzzled about what makes anti-existential claims, like "There are no unicorns", true. There need not be any separate truth-makers

for such a claim; rather it is entailed by the basic existential truths jointly, since there is nothing in the list that is a unicorn, and it says at the end of the list that there is nothing else.

V. The Nature of Proof

1. That the generally accepted current epistemological definition of knowledge is "justified true belief" is attested to by a number of writers whose works are compiled in a (text) book by Louis P. Pohman. Pohman, L.P., (2003). Belmont CA: Wadsworth/Thomson Learning.

VI. The Use of Language

1. There are many more factors that play into how the mind processes information. These include feelings, emotions and other data in the mind. For now we will just deal with the very elemental distinction of a concrete image and an abstract concept.

2. See Endnote #13 in Chapter III.

3. Taken from Wittgenstein's position in Chapter III. See Endnote #9 in Chapter III.

4. Muggeridge, M. (1980). The End of Christendom, Grand Rapids MI: William B. Eerdsman Publishing Co.

Muggeridge (1903-1990) was a renowned English journalist, author of 10 books, a radio and television personality and editor of Punch, the English humor magazine.

See: http://www.nndb.com/people/352/000087091/

IX. Ten Precepts of Dialogue

1. For the most part, these definitions were taken from: The American Heritage Dictionary, Fourth Edition. (2001) New York: Random House, Inc.

2. This paraphrase of Lewis lists additional examples from what Lewis gave. Lewis, C.S. (1952). Mere Christianity, Westwood, NJ: Barbour and Company, Inc.

3. There is no term that encompasses all the data in the mind—images, ideas, concepts and feelings. In order to encompass all these elements in one term we have borrowed the term *mencept* which was coined in Book One in The Way Things Are series. See End Note 3 under Chapter X below.

4. For an extensive review of fallacies go to www.fallacyfiles.org

X. Survey of Literature

1. www.npr.org/templates/story/story.php?storyId= 1248919

2. Van Emeren. F.& Grootendorst, R, (2002). Argumentation, Mahwah NJ: Lawrence Erlbaum Associates, Inc.

3. Hoppins, C. (1997), Basic Precepts of Reality and Common Sense, Boise ID: Western Research Press.

APPENDIX C
SAIKAT GUHA

It is fitting that this book be dedicated to Saikat Guha (1976-2008). Blessed with a brilliant mind, he had an extra-ordinary ability to communicate He was a voracious reader, a storehouse of knowledge and a prolific writer. He had a way of explaining complicated philosophical concepts that made them seem simple. He was a seeker after truth in all his philosophical endeavors and was quick to point out errors in the positions taken in works by major authors and others. The positions he took on various issues are generally sound. It is for this reason he is quoted many times in this text.

Guha was born in Bangladesh and grew up the United States. He grew up a Hindu. He became an atheist, then a Buddhist and still later he embraced Christianity. He was profoundly influenced by Thomas Aquinas and while a graduate student at the University of Washington, he was baptized a Roman Catholic.

He posted some 27 book reviews on Amazon.com while an undergraduate student at Boise State University. He possibly had a photographic memory. In class he did not take notes, but sat focused on what was being said.

His writings have been collected and published in the form of ebooks. As of this writing, three books by Guha in electronic format, containing a collection of his work, were available for downloading on Amazon.com's Kindle.

Among Guha' pearls of wisdom were these:

> In a book review on Quine's Philosophy of Logic, Guha warned, "Don't be seduced into thinking he must be right because he's a genius. There is much to be learned from great philosophers, but uncritical acceptance of their theories is a disastrous policy."

> In a book review of Adler's 10 Philosophical Mistakes, Guha said, "...common sense overdone is a thousand times better than philosophy without common sense."

> Contra to the writings of Wittgenstein and Russell, Guha posted the following note:

>> Sense: Unnecessary. Representational fallacy. (Very pervasive.) No term is empty; an empty term would be meaningless. All terms pick out something, real or otherwise. What terms pick out are objects of thought. So-called "empty" terms just don't pick out anything real, or existent. (This is at http://www.saikatguha.com/logic-and-mathematics/absolute-logic-and-philosophy-of-language-notes)

By extrapolation one can apply this last note to a proposition, a principle, the minimalist theories of truth and probably a lot of other positions.

APPENDIX D
WESTERN RESEARCH
INSTITUTE

Western Research Institute (WRI), has been a provider of research services since 1987. At the time of the publication of this book, WRI was involved in the research, compilation and publishing of a series of books involving the current status of development of certain elements of philosophy and related subjects mainly in the United States, but also in other countries around the world. This series of books is entitled *The Way Things Are*.

This book, the second in this series, provides guidelines for compiling the remaining books in the series. Since the quest of the series is about attaining truth insofar as that is possible, this book (Book Two) sets the standard for dialogue that meets that objective.

While Book Four establishes the concept of a basic philosophy and proposes basic principles of this basic philosophy that everyone can accept with certitude, it does not purport to hold these principles inviolate to further examination and discussion. In fact further discussion and dialogue is necessary to establish their validity or invalidity.

Thus the main purpose, and to which the scope of this book was limited, was to establish a process and provide the means to facilitate dialogue and reconcile disparate positions so that knowledge could be advanced, a greater understanding could be achieved of philosophical questions being debated, greater civility in public discourse could attain, and that peace and harmony could prevail. To this end the tools of discourse and precepts of dialogue have been proffered and belabored.

WRI has been in the process over the past number of years of conducting a poll on what is truth and what makes a thing true. The results of this poll has been published on the WRI web site at www.wrii.org. The importance of these two questions as they relate to communication and other activities is a major theme of this book and does not need further elaboration here. Results of the surveys appear in various chapters of this book.

In addition to compiling and publishing reports and books, WRI was involved in investigative and legal research, and collection of news and opinion with special emphasis on the law, the courts and the legal profession. WRI is an independent reporter of facts. It has no agenda except freedom of information and holding lawmakers and others accountable for what they say for public consumption.

Reports and books compiled by WRI are generally listed on the WRI website at wrii.org. Details of these projects were available at non-public portions of the WRI website to anyone who wished to contribute material to them. A detailed schedule for payment of royalties for contributors to the various projects was also available at non-public portions of the WRI website. They could be accessed by going to wrii.org/forum.

The object of Books in *The Way Things Are* series is to present elemental aspects of philosophy to the general public.

The high degree of sophistication that the writings of professional philosophers has reached is for the most part beyond the ken of the general public. It takes a major in philosophy to even begin to understand the esoteric positions being debated in the philosophical community and much of it was even beyond those philosophy majors who did not go on to post graduate work. Most of the then current writings of professional philosophers were directed at other professional philosophers. *The Way Things Are* series sought to report on a number of theories being debated in a way that is understandable to those who do not have a major in philosophy. In short *The Way Things Are* series is philosophy for the rest of us.

Following is a tentative list in the series along with a general indication of the subject matter:

BOOK ONE: The Basic Precepts of Reality
and Common Sense

The Book That Set The Standard for WRI Reports
(Second Edition)

BOOK TWO: Ten Precepts of Dialogue

Philosophy and Communication
The Tools for Constructive Discourse

BOOK THREE: Reconciling Disparate
Philosophical Systems

The Results of a Multi-Year Study and Polls
The Important Philosophers of The 20th Century

BOOK FOUR: Philosophia Universalis et Perennis

The One True Standard Basic Universal Philosophy
Contra Wittgenstein and Russell

BOOK FIVE: Ontology, Evolution and Creation

How It All Began
What Is Wrong With The Creationism Argument

BOOK SIX: Self Empowerment

A Critique of Books and Belief Systems
What's True, What's False and What Works

BOOK SEVEN: In Search of Reality

Basic Principles
The Foundation of All Knowledge

BOOK EIGHT: In Search of Truth

What Truth Is and What Makes A Thing True
More Than 90 Percent of Adults Can't Articulate It

BOOK NINE: The Defamation of Truth

Dance of the Spin Doctors
How False Information Has Harmed Society

BOOK TEN: Tools of Deception

How People in Power Fool You
The Fallacies, Guides to Discernment

BOOK ELEVEN: A Layman's Guide to Logic

The Foundation of All Disciplines
How To Master The Art of Critical Thinking

BOOK TWELVE: The Basic Principles
of Morality and Ethics

Why There Needs To Be A Standard
The Basis of Social Well Being

Book One was published in 1998. A Second edition is in the works. Book Two is this book. Considerable work has been done on Books Three, Five and Six. A date for their publishing has not been set. Book Four may get published toward the end of this year (2016) or the following year. The remaining books in the series are still in the conception stage and their order in the series and their titles are not set in concrete. Contributions to all books in the series are invited, even those in publication stage as all books were to continue to be revised, updated and added to, and a Ph.D. is not required for a contribution or manuscript to be accepted and published.

Contributions to or criticisms of books already published are especially solicited since content is continually being revised and data for subsequent editions is continually being collected.

As time progresses, things change. Web sites are taken down, addresses and phone numbers change, companies are acquired by other companies or go out of business or move and their presence on the Internet changes accordingly or disappears. WRI is a non-profit Idaho corporation and has been in continuous existence since 1987. Information on its past, present and future existence can be obtained on the business entities section of the Idaho Secretary of State web site.

APPENDIX E
TRIVIA

Editors before the computer age needed to have a large vocabulary with a comprehensive knowledge of spelling. With spell-check that is not as important as it once was.

In writing and/or publishing a book, the author and/or publisher gets to do things not otherwise available to writers and/or publisher in other venues such as magazines or newspapers.

There are choices not available in another venue such as style and the use of different forms of expression. In the matter of spelling one has the choice of British or American. Word processing programs in America generally use the American spelling in their spell-check, but not always. At least one version of Microsoft Word uses at least some British spelling. Examples are color versus colour, center versus centre, labor versus labour, favor versus favour, traveled versus travelled, encyclopedia versus encyclopaedia, baptise versus baptize and many more.

In the matter of style there are more than half a dozen different organizations that publish style books. Among them are the American Psychological Association (APA), the

Modern Language Association (MLA), The Associated Press (AP), the Chicago Manual of Style (CMS) and many more.

This book uses the American Psychological Association style book for citations and The Associated Press style book for everything else.

Each generation seems to need to change things for the sake of change in the belief that their generation is more knowledgeable than the previous generation. Such is the use of C.E., Christian Era and B.C.E., Before the Christian Era, in place of A.D. Anno Domini (Year of *Our* Lord) and B.C., Before Christ, which occurred in the last half of the 20th Century.

It exemplifies the trend in modernism and post modernism and the need for political correctness and the need to disassociate scholarly research from religious tradition.

Just to be contrary we have chosen to use the politically incorrect form of B.C. and A.D. in this treatise.

While vast amounts of knowledge is gained with each new generation, what is often overlooked is vast amounts of knowledge is also lost.

Tear out..
The Ten Precepts of Dialogue are:

I. Everybody has a right to his position and to change it and the right to raise an issue (make a statement).

I (the communicator) have a right to my position.
I have a right to change my position.
I have a right to raise an issue.

II. Any communicator has the right to state and define a position and the obligation to defend a position or statement(s) (provide proof of their truth or validity).

I (the communicator) have the right to state and define my position.

I (the communicator) must (I have the obligation to) provide proof of the truth of my statement and/or the validity of my position.

III. The persons being communicated to (the communicatees) have the obligation to themselves, to the person making a statement or maintaining a position and to society to correctly understand and accept the statement or position being communicated.

You (the communicatee) must (You have the obligation to) understand and accept my position and/or statement (that it is legitimate).

This also gives the right of the communicatee to question the communicator.

IV. Any person has a right to disagree with the position and/or statement of any other person and to question that person.

I (the communicator) have a right to disagree with you.
You (the communicatee) have a right to disagree with me.
I have a right to question you.
You have a right to question me.

V. The person maintaining a position has a right to verify that all his statements and his position are correctly understood.

I (the communicator) have a right to verify that you understand what I am saying.

VI. The person making a statement or maintaining a position has the obligation and the right to distinguish and define (within the rules of logic) the terms and concepts he uses.

I (the communicator) have the right to define the terms and concepts I use in explaining my position.

VII. All those involved in *dialogue* have the obligation to accept and use the terms and concepts as defined by the person advancing a position.

You (the communicatee) must accept my definition of the terms and concepts I use.

VIII. All parties have the obligation to distinguish between a person and the position of that person.

You (the communicatee) must distinguish between me and my position and the statements I make..

IX. All parties have the obligation to not impute to another person beliefs, knowledge, ignorance, feelings, thoughts, intentions, positions or any other thing.

You have no right to impute (that particular thing).

X. All parties have the obligation to abide by certain principles of reality, the laws of thought and certain principles and rules of logic and identification of fallacies.

You must abide by (state a particular principle, rule, law or fallacy).

www.ingramcontent.com/pod-product-compliance
Lightning Source LLC
Chambersburg PA
CBHW031555040426
42452CB00006B/308